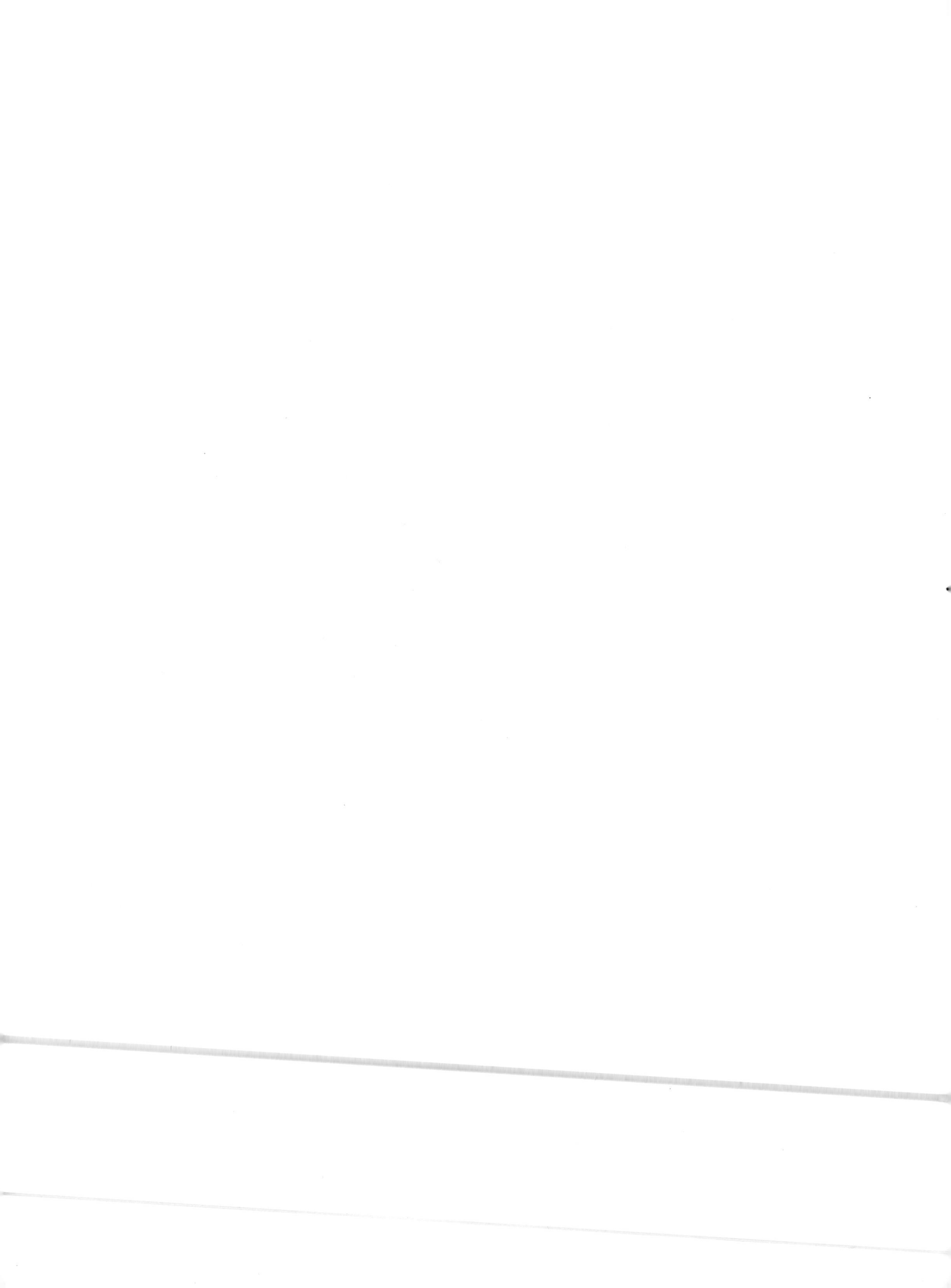

HOFFMAN, OKMULGEE COUNTY, OKLAHOMA

Doing Business on The Indian Territory Frontier

by

Mickey J. "Mike" Martin

THE FOWBLE PRESS

PUBLICATION DATA

ISBN 978-0-9638279-2-0 (Hardback)
Updated – January 1997
Updated – February 2010
Updated – August 2021

LCCN 95060134

****

CONTENTS

CHAPTER I

THE LURE OF THE LAND

What was day-to-day life really like for those who sought economic opportunity during the years following the Great Oklahoma Land Rush in what was until only shortly before the government-protected and still somewhat mysterious Indian Territory? Who were some of the people who stayed on to make a living after the initial euphoria of the period wore off, and what happened to them over the years? What became of those who started businesses, cultivated farms, built up ranches, or entered trades, professions, and crafts during those heady times? Using introductory historical overviews, selected documents, unique and special photographs, and brief recitations of personal experiences of residents of one Land Rush townsite--the town of Hoffman in Okmulgee County--this book attempts to shed additional light by answering questions of this kind.

Most of those who took part in the Great Land Rush episode of our Nation's history were drawn to the Oklahoma frontier in search of economic opportunity, the potential for entrepreneurship, and what must be called a "spirit of adventure." Regardless of the many and varied individual reasons that drew them to the area, an overriding desire for freedom to pursue personal economic self-interest was the universal guiding light.

Many of the events that make up the history of the Great Land Rush period of the State of Oklahoma and this part of America's period of western expansion were lived out by the original settlers and subsequent residents of rural communities such as Hoffman Townsite, the small town featured in this book as being generally representative of the collective experience of many of the settlers. There were real people behind the events that make up this history, people who did the best they could with what they had to build solid futures for their families. Their lives would surely have seemed unremarkable at the time, but today their experiences are at the same time fascinating as well as historically interesting. They do not seem boring, not to people living the insulated, comfortable lives most of us do today.

Lessons learned from what happened in places like Hoffman Townsite can indeed help us deal more effectively with the economic, political, social and moral issues of life today. Imaginative but fictitious stories about frontier life may be entertaining, but they are never as helpful in terms of dealing with the vicissitudes of real life as the unvarnished truth. Places such as Hoffman were not the stuff of dreams, nor were they accidental events; they were historical episodes in which men and women acted out their lives just as they do today. Benefit can be derived from reconsidering the basic values that drove economic life in those times. Some of the spirit that propelled people back then is more than worthy of understanding and emulation today, and we can learn a great deal by carefully considering their successes as well as their mistakes.

Many rural towns of 100 years ago were devastated when our nation went through a relatively rapid transition from an agricultural to an industrial economy. By studying the economic experience of townsites such as Hoffman and others like it, we can build insights that can help us deal with the most significant transition of our own times--the even more bewildering change from an industrial to an information society. Will we, for example, be wise enough today to reverse the appalling and disastrous loss of human potential and the blight of area after area that is taking place in our central cities? And, most of all, can we move toward the development of prosperous business centers populated by self-sufficient people in these areas? All this remains to be seen, given that today many of our cities are struggling to cope with the same fundamental problems of inadequate basic economic opportunity and public support services that in their day led to the demise of small farm towns like Hoffman.

To appreciate the true beauty of a town like Hoffman and to understand why people were drawn to it as a place to settle, it is necessary to learn something about its history. Like any other place, the better it is known the more alive it becomes, beginning with understanding that the town itself was, in effect, a business. Without a picture of what it was really like and some appreciation of the historical events that gave rise to its existence, it is all too easy to minimize the role it and other towns like it played in national history.

The combined adverse impact of economic industrialization, the Great Depression and Dust Bowl episodes, traumatic local events, and natural disasters such as fire and the tornado of 1960 eventually wound up being too much for the town of Hoffman to overcome. Today, only a few homes and businesses are clearly recognizable from its relatively prosperous early days. Looking at what does remain, however, can still bring a lump to the throats of those who know what the town once was and understand what it might have become.

Due to the impact of the period on the formation of our collective character and values, Hoffman and townsites like it should be remembered with accuracy, clarity, and full understanding. Anything less would devalue and diminish this important period in history. The settlers and former residents of places like Hoffman Townsite were the human legacy of the Great Oklahoma Land Rush. They were the people who remained after the initial euphoria of those times wore off, and their experience was abundantly representative of the lives of thousands of residents of many other small towns that dotted the State during the early 1900s.

Experiences varied widely town by town and person by person, but many residents of Oklahoma's land boom townsites—like towns themselves, with Hoffman being no exception—clearly struggled for survival rather than continued upward in terms of sustained economic prosperity. Examining the story of Hoffman as an example of a "boomer" townsite is an effective means of developing a more realistic and complete understanding of the economic experiences of ordinary people during the period of highly speculative land and town development that followed on the heels of Oklahoma's Great Land Rush.

While we can never go home again, we can educate ourselves to recognize, remember, and even to feel the special part of our national heritage that was the lives of our forefathers--those who actually experienced the period depicted in this story of one small farm town. In our world of work and striving and challenge, it is good to recall with all the respect that the period rightfully deserves the uniqueness of places like Hoffman Townsite. That is what this book is all about-- recounting what life in Hoffman was like back in its early days to remind us of what average people had to deal with to make a living in the many townsites that sprang up during Oklahoma's Great Land Rush days. There were many such places in Oklahoma's history, and without such a record not much remains to tell this part of the story. And it is a story very much worth the telling, for what happened in the life of Hoffman Townsite is, in a way, the story of the entire State of Oklahoma and, in fact, of the United States of America.

Some of Oklahoma's land rush townsites succeeded beyond any-one's expectations, but many went through a period of great struggle just to survive. And many of them, in fact, did not survive. Hoffman, for example, jumped to a promising start, and then eventually all but died. In the process, however, it became the base of experience on which many went on to build happy and successful lives. It is good now to look back on its story and to realize the role this time period played in building our national consciousness, and to understand--for many perhaps for the first time--that those who lived back then were part of a proud but fleeting moment in one of the key stages of our national economic history. Realizing these things enables us to look back on their experience with respect and pride, knowing in ways not easy to express that their lives mattered a great deal to all of us. Let us, therefore, take a brief look back in time to get to know some of the people who started businesses and otherwise earned a livelihood in Hoffman and to review some of the achievements that made up its history as a townsite on the Oklahoma Land Rush frontier.

Counties and County Seats of the State of Oklahoma

Okmulgee and McIntosh Counties in the State of Oklahoma

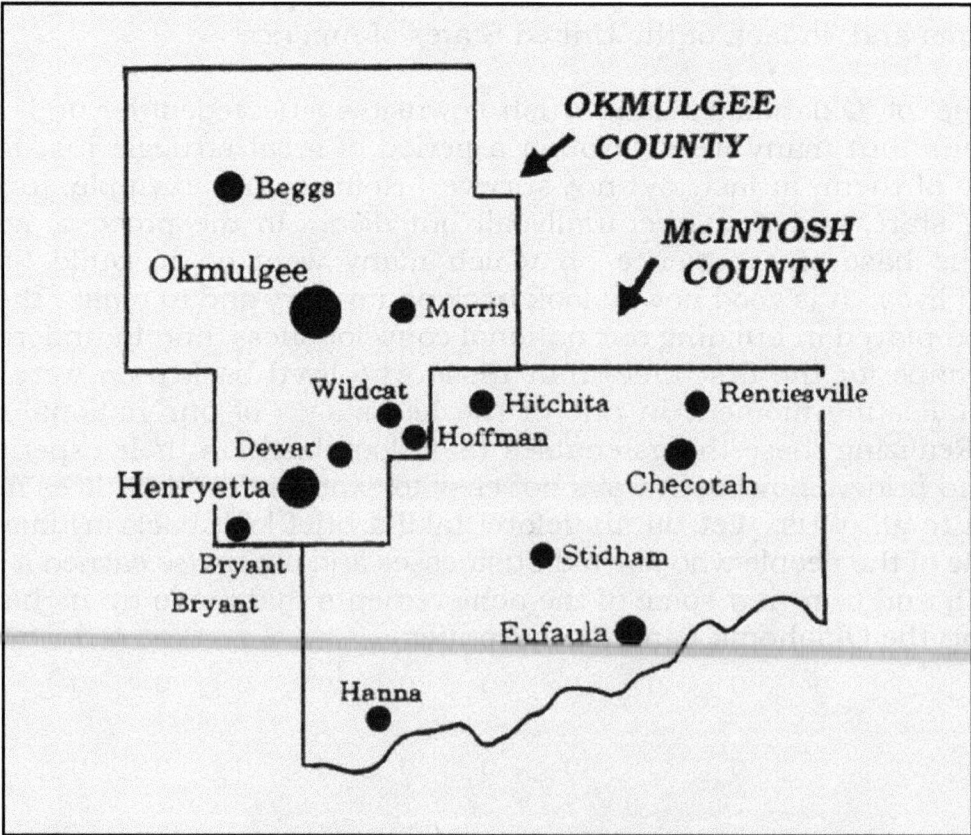

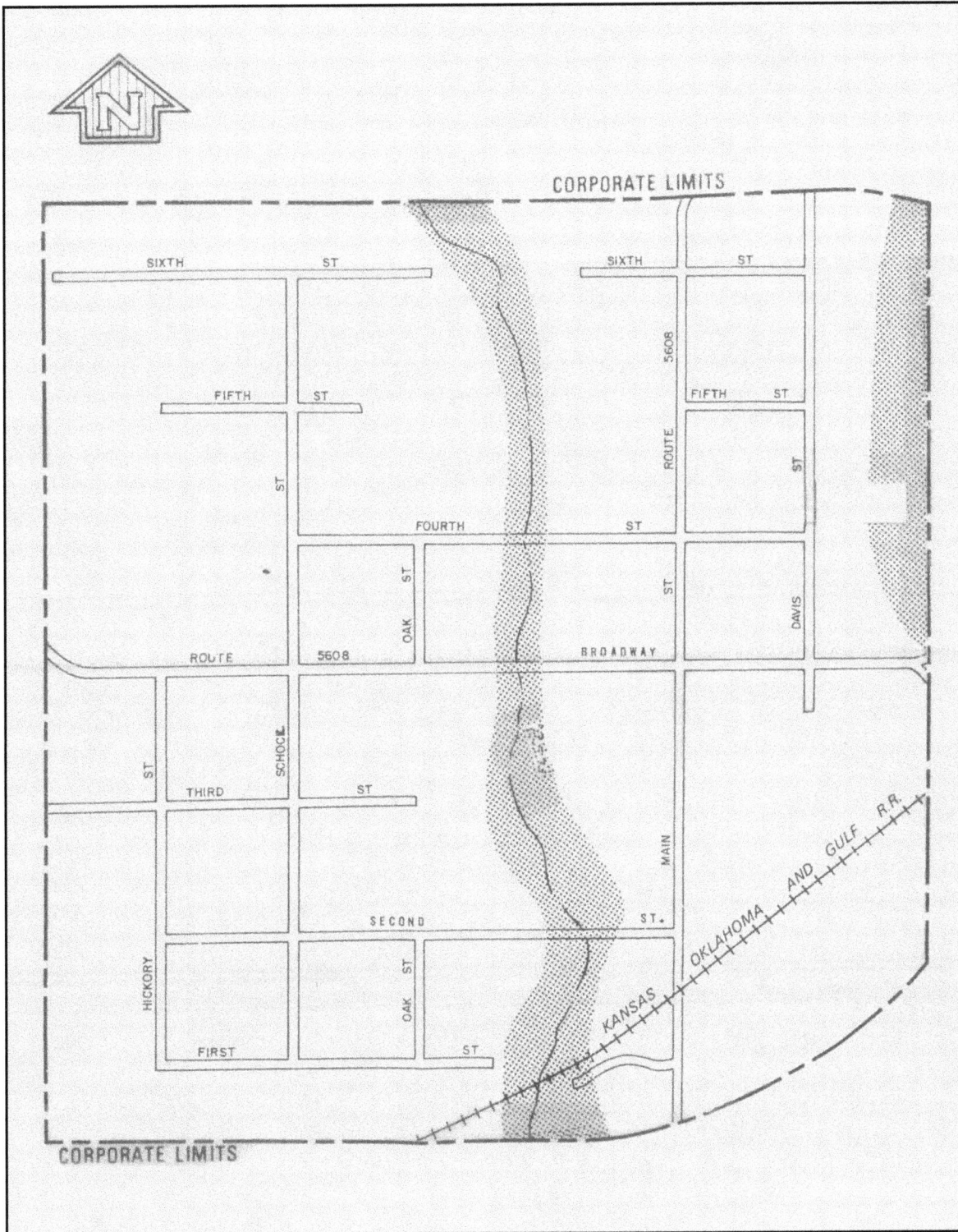

Present day street map of the Village of Hoffman
in Okmulgee County, Oklahoma

CHAPTER II

THE
INDIAN TERRITORY
PERIOD

INTRODUCTION

The record shows that before it was settled, the area around what was to become Hoffman Townsite was fertile and green and full of natural game. Grass for grazing animals was plentiful and there were large groves of trees in creek and river bottom lands. There was a profusion of plant and animal life, including stands of commercially harvestable timber.

There were coal, oil, and natural gas reserves in the ground, and ample water in the local creeks and rivers. Due to a high annual rainfall, the area stayed green for most of the year. Stretching away to the south of the area that eventually became the center of Hoffman for five or six miles was a strip of heavily timbered land where acres of oak trees grew untouched by man. Much of the area was rich, well-watered, bottom land capable of growing many kinds of plants and trees. To the north and east lay thousands of acres of rolling, black sandy prairie land covered with bluestem grass from three to five feet high. To the immediate south and west were a range of small hills, then more rolling grass land.

According to some who have studied the subject, as many as 225,000 Indians belonging to many different tribes lived in the area that is now the central part of continental United States. Most of the original Indians who lived in what is now Oklahoma were not primarily farmers, but hunters who relied heavily on the abundance of game animals found in their unordered and sparsely populated area of the country. Unlike some of the southeastern tribes, even those who kept semi-permanent villages and raised some garden crops still most likely wandered far and wide to hunt for game. Wild game was the principal source of their food, clothing, and shelter.

The native Indians of the area did not conceive of themselves as landowners but as land users. In fact, they did not believe that anyone had a right to "own" the land, waterways, or the privilege of hunting wild game. They believed that man should be free to wander wherever his strengths and interests might take him. Unfortunately, the whites who later entered Indian lands in search of homesteads interpreted the very attitudes and values of the Indians themselves to mean that Native American areas were unclaimed and, therefore, available to anyone who settled them. Before the Indians truly understood what was happening to them and began to organize an effective resistance, most of their land was lost forever.

RESETTLEMENT OF THE SOUTHEASTERN CREEK INDIANS NEAR HOFFMAN

Settlement of the general area around Hoffman and of Hoffman Townsite in particular with a fixed population began when the federal government forcibly moved--or "resettled," as it was put back then--the southeastern Creek Indians of Alabama, Georgia, and the Carolinas to the area during the 1800s. To truly understand the development of Hoffman Townsite, it is necessary to know something of this historical episode and the role the Creek Indians played in the early growth and development of the area. That story begins with an explanation of how the Creeks came to be resettled in Oklahoma in the first place. One of the best accounts of this event has been provided by Michael D. Green in an excellent study called "The Politics of Indian Removal," an overview of which is the principal reference for the following pages of this chapter.

There had been a long relationship between the Creek people and the white explorers, traders, and settlers of our country's pioneer period before the tribe was removed to Oklahoma, but it was never a particularly happy one. Long before they were forced out of their native homelands in Alabama, Georgia, and parts of the Carolinas, the Creeks had in several significant ways been negatively impacted by their contact with whites. As was the case with other Indian tribes, for example, their lack of immunity to diseases such as smallpox, measles, influenza, and others caused them misery and death at a level we can hardly imagine today.

The very earliest explorers to Creek tribal areas in the southwestern United States recorded that "there had been a pest in the land" and that everywhere there were "large, vacant towns, grown up in grass." When Fernando DeSoto's men arrived years later, they too afflicted the Indians with illnesses for which they had no immunities. Twenty years after some of their earliest contacts with whites, the western part of the original Creek territory, which as far back as the 1540s had been densely settled, was nearly depopulated. Even further contacts with Spanish and other European explorers, traders, settlers, and missionaries in the sixteenth and seventeenth centuries meant that disease continued to take a toll on these Indians through the years that followed.

It has been estimated that regional epidemics occurring in 1696-98, 1738-39, 1759-60, 1779-80, and as late as 1831 killed off a huge number of the Native Indian population of the southeastern United States. At no time before removal from their native homelands were the Creeks ever free of epidemic diseases of one kind or another caused by their contact with whites. In fact, some researchers have estimated that as many as nineteen out of twenty Native Indians died of epidemic diseases within the first two centuries of their contact with whites. (As shown by the following letter, Native American Indian's experienced problems of this kind even up until relatively current times.)

Once the explorations of DeSoto and others paved the way, more whites of various nationalities moved into the areas once occupied only by the southeastern Creeks. By 1700, Creek Indians were in direct and frequent contact with Spanish settlers in Florida, French settlers in Louisiana, and British settlers in the Carolinas. At first the relationship between the Indians and whites seemed to be mutually beneficial

During these early years, economics dominated the relations between natives and whites. Both sides actively pursued trade and both benefited, at least initially, from the barter of deer hides and captives for guns, powder, and the manufactured goods whites used as trade items. For the Creeks, however, the full ramifications of their interaction with whites became apparent only after a long association with it.

One of the most basic changes that affected Creek society had to do with the acquisition of manufactured goods. The iron and steel tools and weapons traded by the whites for deerskins, furs, and captives dramatically changed the way Creek men spent their time. For example, handmade deerskin clothing was replaced by cloth clothing and guns replaced bows and arrows for use in hunting and fighting.

What ultimately happened was that Creek reliance on the new trade goods provided by the whites becomes a dependence so debilitating that they lost their ability to defend their territory when the expansionist demands of the whites began to grow. The time released by the great reduction in labor hours devoted to hand making domestic goods wound up being absorbed by a major increase in the production of deer hides, the Creek nation's principal medium of exchange in trade, and by increased warfare on neighboring tribes to acquire captives for the slave market. Hides and slaves were the major items the Creeks traded to whites to get the manufactured goods they wanted.

When Creek men hunted only for their own food, they stayed relatively close to their home area. But when their appetite for manufactured goods started to grow, Creek hunters had to spend more time hunting and to travel further from home to find deer. This had the effect of increasing their contacts with tribes that lived near them and having to compete with them for a finite number of deer.

The profit motive introduced by white traders also changed the very nature of Creek warfare. At one time, they had fought against other Indians only sporadically and in retaliation for offenses against the nation. The Creeks now began to make large-scale invasions into the territories of other tribes for the sole purpose of capturing prisoners to be sold to slave traders. The profits of slaving were enough to make the business worthwhile, but it has been estimated that as many as three Indians died for each one captured for slavery. Creek men became, in effect, commercial hunters and slave raiders, and became less and less involved with agriculture and other domestic affairs.

Most Creek towns during these early years of contact with whites had one or more white traders in residence. They built stores and houses, kept herds of cattle, horses, and hogs, married Creek women, and raised bilingual and bicultural mixed-blood children. For most of the year the trader sold goods on credit, collecting payment in tanned hides in the spring. Creek trade centered around replacing items they formerly hand-made by themselves with manufactured goods made by whites.

As time passed, relations between the Creeks and whites became strained over the Creek leaders' concern with unregulated and unethical traders and unrestrained squatters moving into their territory. The state and federal governments of that time made some relatively token attempts to deal with these problems, but the pressure from white settlers, traders, and politicians was such that they found it an almost hopeless task. White leaders in Alabama and Georgia were far more interested in doing whatever they could to take land away from the native Indians than in protecting their rightful claims to it.

Many whites of that time were contemptuous of the native Indians and their property rights, and some were downright cruel, dishonest, and greedy in their relations with them. Most of the traders did not respect the Indians nor were they in turn respected, but they put up with each other because both sides mutually benefited from their trade relationships. The Indians came to look upon any whites in their territory that were of no benefit to them as enemies whose encroachments and abuses demanded resistance.

However legitimate they may have been, the complaints of the Creeks against the early white settlers and traders in their homelands were met more with platitudes than with any real solutions. Land was the real issue, and the only interaction whites were really interested in was for the Creeks to sell off their land for legal occupation by settlers and developers. White leaders creatively plotted and schemed to find ways to get the Indians off their land. Little by little, Creek headmen began to sell or barter away pieces of land in exchange for peace and quiet and basic personal safety. Whatever they did, however, was never enough; the white settlers wanted it all.

Ultimately realizing that white encroachment would be a perpetual and ever-increasing threat to their independence and territorial claims, Creek leaders tried to rally their people into a stronger tribal association that would give them some protection against white expansionism. The Creek Indians of Georgia and Alabama eventually did successfully organize their independent and autonomous tribes into a Confederacy that developed some of the attributes of a true national government. Political dissention, however, kept them from ever becoming as effective as they could have been.

Knowing that their people were threatened with prospect of literally being inundated by white settlers, Creek leaders did all they could to protect their people and preserve their values and way of life. They fought for concessions, stalled for time during negotiations with whites, and fought to bridge the gaps between the many factions and special interest groups that existed among their own people. Factionalism, disunity, particularism, obsessive local loyalties, however, all combined to drain the Nation's strength in terms of dealing with the encroachment of the whites.

Eventually, the Creeks came to believe that the only way to deal with the whites was to learn from their culture, especially their political organization, and to make adaptions necessary to coexist with the more powerful white culture and institutions. By building a strong, single-minded Creek Nation, they believed they could protect their land and stop the influx of white settlers. They won some time and many concessions for their people, but ultimately a diminished sense of clan community and the introduction of "civilized" concepts had the effect of breaking down Creek tribal unity and creating a spirit of individuality that added to the internal weakness of their Nation.

The Creeks were at least partly forced into a position of having to adopt white ways. In the face of the possibility of being overwhelmed by whites, many hunters followed the lead of the mixed-blood members of their tribe and the advice of government agents and adopted some form of plow agriculture. Those unwilling or unable to make this transition attempted to live on annuity income derived from the land sales. Many, however, steadfastly opposed efforts to make them plow farmers, just as they opposed anything that might put them in a position of having white civilization forced on them.

In those days, even the whites who felt genuine concern for their plight felt a paternalistic moral and economic imperative to promote civilization among the Indians. As far as the state and federal governments of the day were concerned, however, civilization meant plow agriculture practiced on small, individually owned plots of land. The prevailing belief of the time was that "the earth was given to mankind to support the greatest number of which it is capable, and no tribe or people have a right to withhold from the wants of others more than is necessary for their own support and comfort." In other words, the prevailing view among whites was that the Creeks had no right to claim continued ownership of land that they did not settle and farm.

Believing that training native people in plow agriculture would release thousands of acres of "surplus" land for white settlement, Congress enacted the Civilization Fund Act of 1819. The law provided funds for the instruction of Native people "in the mode of agriculture suited to their situation, and for teaching their children in reading, writing, and arithmetic." The true purpose of the civilization law, however, was to make it possible for the government to, in effect, "educate Native people off their land." In pursuit of this goal, the government provided funding to missionary societies to help pay for the construction and maintenance of new Indian schools and to pay the salaries of teachers. In return for this it was understood that the missionaries would support government measures designed to deal with the tribes. Through this unspoken system, the mission societies effectively became semi-official agencies of the federal government.

Contrary to what state and federal government officials had expected, the "civilization" policy worked out very well in terms of the interests of the Indians but not well at all in terms of their own desires. As the Indians became educated according to white laws and standards and became more interested in participating in the economic system of the whites, they became more adept at resisting the manipulations of government efforts focused on depriving them of their land. "Civilized" Indians, in effect, came to understand the true value of their land and resisted efforts to part them from it.

This turn of events became a double-edged sword for white people. They thought that educating the Indians would eventually help get them off their land, but instead it acted to increase their resistance. Frustrated by this turn of events, some white leaders began to advocate a more direct means of opening Indian land for white settlement--denying the sovereignty of the Indian nations, scrapping the treaty system, imposing full congressional control, and condemning Indian lands through the exercise of eminent domain. Justifying their views by claiming a need to protect whites from Indian attacks, white leaders effectively argued that the military security of the southwest region needed a permanent population of whites who would be able to defend it. Military leaders of the day complained that if "the Indians are the subjects of the United States inhabiting its territory and acknowledging its sovereignty, then is it not absurd for the sovereign to negotiate by treaty with the subject?" Native people were "entitled to the protection and fostering care" of the government, but no more so than American citizens. These "citizens" were, therefore, subject to the laws of Congress, just like everybody else.

The Creeks were effectively being forced into accepting land allotments, then manipulated into either giving up or selling for a pittance their land allotment rights and being "removed" to the far west to land where they could finally be free from harassment by whites. Creeks leaders, however, did not support the sale of their land or the idea of moving to an unknown area west of the Mississippi. The Creek Council refused to renegotiate their land rights as provided by existing treaties, and instead demanded their enforcement as promised.

The Creeks pleaded with the government to expel "illegal" squatters from their treaty land, but instead the squatters only became more insistent. For the federal and state government officials of the time, the route of escape from the complaints and controversy stemming from friction between settlers and the Indians lay in the removal of the Creeks to the West. Many considered the protective clauses of the various Indian treaties with contempt, even considering the various land allotment plans under consideration at the time to be little more than elaborate bribes to the headmen and families of the Creek Nation to get the Indians off their land. They fully expected the Creeks, once they had their allotments, to immediately sell them to whites, pocket the money, and leave the area.

No one expected or wanted the Creeks to stay in their home areas as independent land-owning citizens of the states. What the whites really wanted was for the Creeks to voluntarily "remove" from their homeland to be resettled beyond the Mississippi River in areas that were wild, unsettled, and, at that time, unwanted and unclaimed by anyone other than the government. Most of the Creeks probably had no interest in becoming permanent citizens of the white southern states, but neither did they wish to give up their land and leave for an uncertain future in what to them was an unknown place.

Since it would not accomplish their overall objective if only small groups of Creeks agreed to give up their land while the majority wanted to stay put, white officials became more and more frustrated with the Indian situation. Not willing to patiently wait for a better solution, whites did all they could to dislodge the Indians from their land. Eventually, they provoked certain groups of Indians into hostility in order to justify military intervention to break what they had seen as a stalemate in terms of dealing with the "Indian problem."

Little by little with the passage of time, bits and pieces of Indian land were wrested away until it came to a point where the whole of their remaining land was individual property and they had little or no bargaining power left as an independent nation. The Indian people were still there, but their national land rights were gone. Their communal land had become "individual property" in the hands of the whites, a concept that only a few of the Creeks really understood and truly supported. Most of the Creeks were eventually forced into homelessness and near starvation.

Whether it was starvation or frustration that finally sparked the war that followed, the result of it was that the Creek Indians were finally forced to move to land set aside for them west of the Mississippi River. Soldiers and militiamen were ordered "for the suppression of hostilities in the Creek country" to demand the "unconditional submission of the Indians" so that they could be disarmed and "resettled" as fast as this could be accomplished. Whether hostile or friendly, all Creeks were to be transported west--by military force if necessary.

The army accomplished in a few months what politicians and treaty talks had failed for many years to achieve. Their defeat in the Creek War of 1813-14 ended the military power of the south-eastern Creek Indians. From 1814 to 1836, the year of their final removal to the west, the Creek Indians were under continual pressure from the Georgia, Alabama, and United States governments to give up their native homelands. Their defeat in the war and the growing power of white settlers made further armed resistance impossible, and the Creeks (like many other eastern tribes) were forced to leave their home area for resettlement in the newly created Oklahoma Indian Territory.

The United States Government forcibly removed the Creek tribe, along with four other so-called "civilized" tribes, over the "Trail of Tears" to "Indian Territory," or what is now Eastern Oklahoma. The first forced migration occurred in 1828, the second in 1832, and the third in 1836. Five or more groups, a total of around 19,609 Creeks, were eventually resettled in the new land, of which the federal War Department classified around 2,500 as "hostile." Only a few Creeks were left in their native area. Hundreds of those who were resettled died of hunger, disease, and exposure before their trip west was completed. Those who did reach Indian Territory were settled in what is now the State of Oklahoma, ragged and downcast in spirit.

The new Creek Indian Nation was situated within the area that later became McIntosh, Muskogee, Okmulgee, and Tulsa counties of Oklahoma. The area that is now the town of Okmulgee, named after Ocmulgee, Georgia, where the Creeks had lived since before recorded history, eventually became their national capitol. In their new area, the tribe was established as what was essentially an independent nation within the border of the United States.

Once established in their new home in Oklahoma, the Creeks lived as citizens of their own sovereign if not actually totally independent nation. They made their own laws, saw to their own law enforcement, conducted government operations, and generally carried on as any small country would. As their new area became more established, trading posts and then small settlements began to form in various locations. It was one of these clusters that eventually grew into the town of Hoffman.

By law, the land areas set aside for the various resettled tribes as "Indian Territory" were to be protected in perpetuity from settlement by outsiders. The treaties the federal government had signed with the Indians gave tribes like the Creeks rights supposedly parallel with those of independent nations, with territorial borders that were to be respected as well as protected.

Even so, white and black settlers illegally pushed their way into Indian territory, ignoring their legitimate treaties and rights. And all through the 1850s powerful interest groups such as cattlemen and railroad companies pressured the federal government to open any and all specifically unassigned areas in the region for access and development. Confusing the situation even more, some of the resettled tribes leased land to the federal government in the southwestern area of present-day Oklahoma for use as hunting grounds for tribes of plains Indians and other lands to settlers for use as ranches and farms. The various Indian agencies kept records of these transactions.

For various reasons, the federal government could not (and some say would not) protect the Indians and their lands. Indians leaders had come to clearly realize what the intrusion of white settlers would mean to their own race and to their claims against the land, but they lacked the political power to change the course of events taking place before their very eyes.

THE GREAT
LAND RUSH OPPORTUNITY

Numerous boundary and jurisdictional changes occurred in Oklahoma over the years. Congress bought the area known as the Panhandle Strip in 1850, but it was separate from Oklahoma or any state and was called "No Man's Land." It was in 1854 that Congress confined Indian Territory to the present-day State of Oklahoma (except for the Panhandle Strip).

When the Civil War ended in 1866, the federal government insisted that the resettled Indian tribes renegotiate their land treaties as compensation for the fact that Indians for the most part had sided with the South against the North during the war. One reason for renegotiating the treaties is that doing so would clear the way to open more land for white settlement and, at the same time, make room for the government to settle black slaves newly freed as a result of the Civil War. Even though the overall amount of land set aside for reservations was reduced by means of the new treaties, even more Indian tribes were resettled there in the years that followed. And even after these changes, the so-called "Cherokee Strip" on the northern border and a much-valued area in the center of Oklahoma were still not assigned a specific use--they were therefore called "unassigned lands." Prospective settlers began to call these areas--and, in fact, all Indian Territory--"the promised land" due to the opportunity it offered for excellent livestock grazing and the possibility of free land for homesteading.

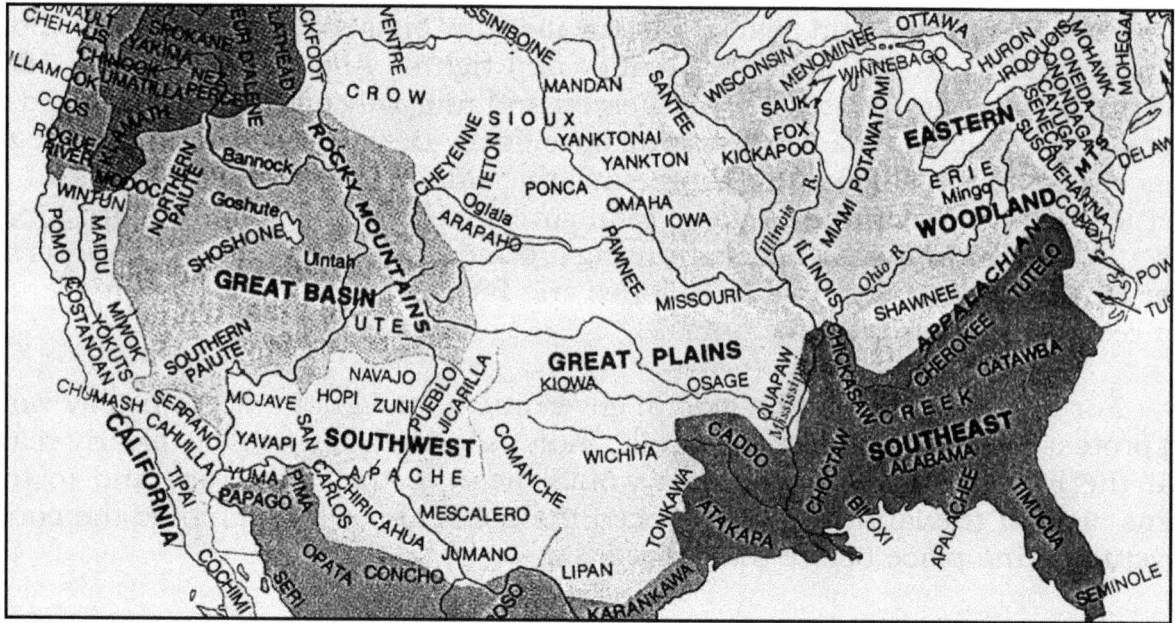

Original Creek Tribal Homelands in Alabama, Florida And Georgia. Map covers from about 1250 A.D. to 1900 A.D. Not all of the Indian groups shown lived in the same time period—some developed at a later date.
Source: Land of Promise: A History of the United States From 1865.

Oklahoma Indian Territory from 1844 To 1865
Source: Oklahoma Place Names by George H. Shirk

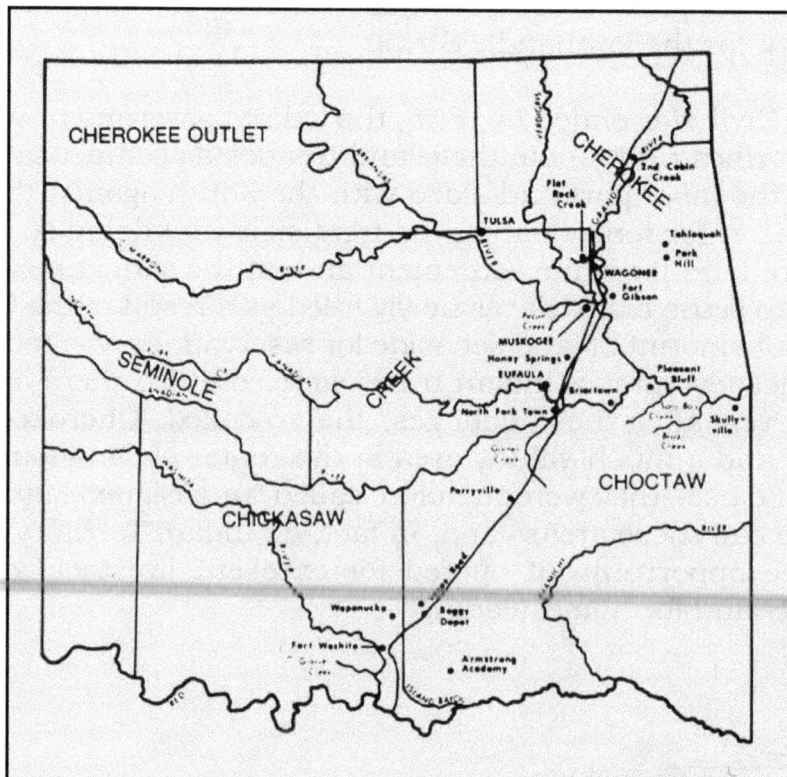

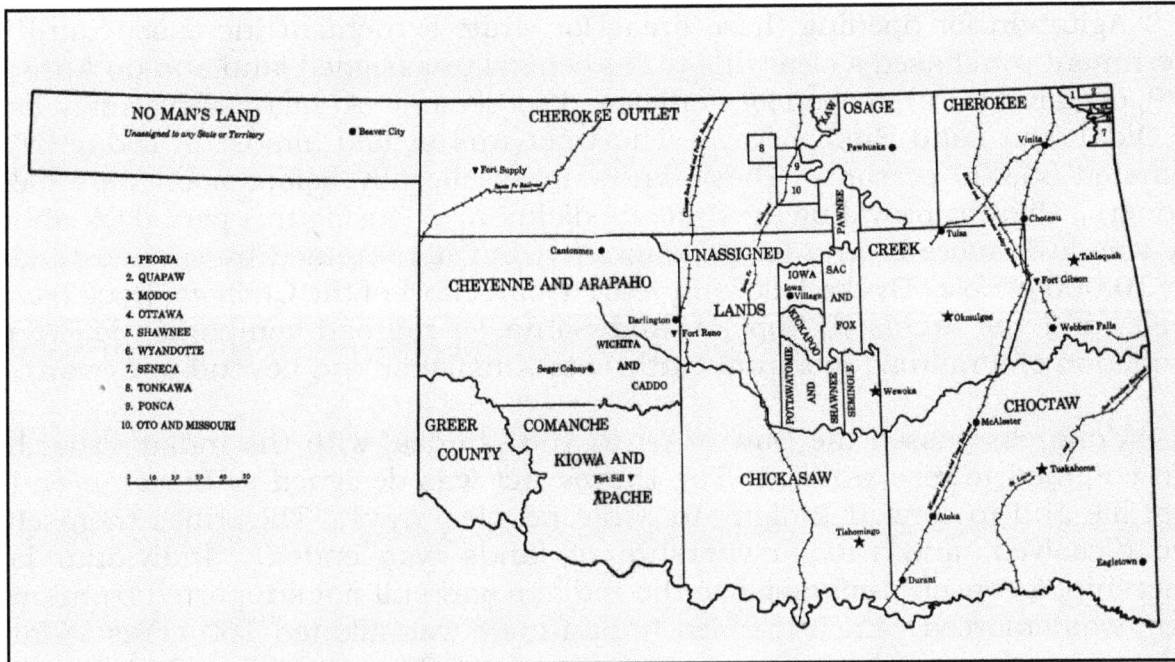

TOP: *Oklahoma Indian Territory from 1866 to 1889*

BOTTOM: *The Creek Indian Nation in 1898*
Source: *Oklahoma Place Names by George H. Shirk*

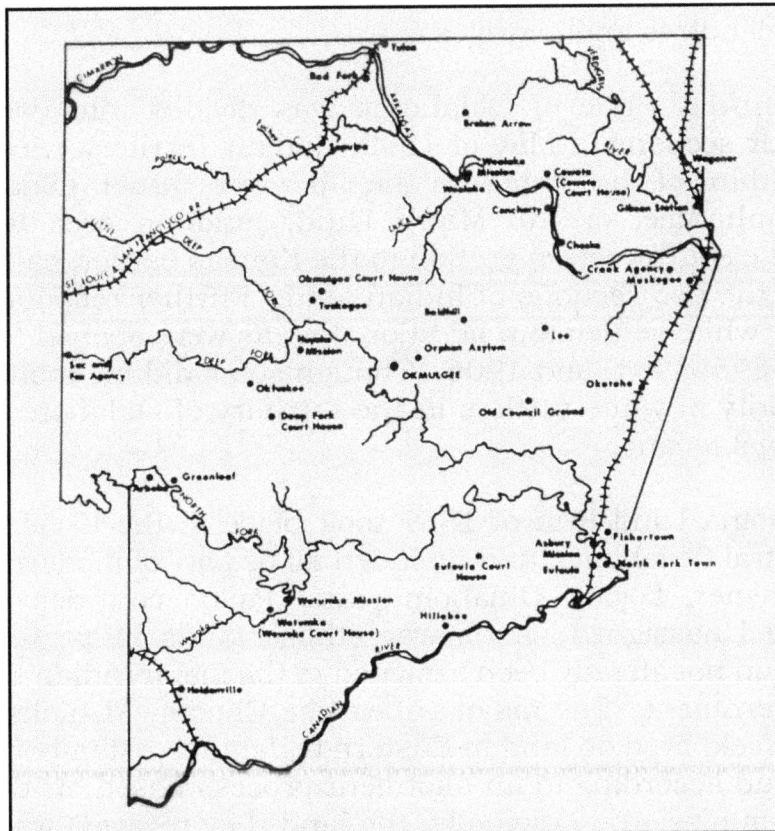

Agitation for opening these areas for white settlement increased until the government purchased a clear title to the central unassigned land and on April 22, 1889, declared the area open for homestead settlement. At high noon on that date, the Oklahoma Land Rush began. The tract was settled almost in a day by an estimated 50,000 persons. Those who entered illegally before noon were called "Sooners," thereby providing the State its nickname. During this period Oklahoma City was little more than a tent community, but it contained by some estimates over 10,000 people. By the following year, a joint effort of the Chicago, Rock Island, Pacific, and the Atchison, Topeka, and Santa Fe railroad companies led to the completion of a railroad line from Guthrie to Kingfisher and beyond to Seward.

Congress passed the Dawes Act in 1887 to deal with the Indians that had been confined to reservations. The Dawes Act was designed to bring an end to tribal life and to convert Indians to white peoples' ways. The tribes themselves were dissolved, and tribal ownership of lands was ended. Individual land ownership, a concept unfamiliar to the Indians and still not supported by many of them, was enforced. Each married Indian male was allotted 160 acres to farm, while each adult single man or woman received 80 acres. Freed blacks were considered "adoptees" of the various tribes to justify giving them the same kinds of land allotments that were given to the Indians. Allottees were given the right to resell or transfer their land rights, and the Dawes Act also made it possible for non-Indians to settle on land that was not allotted to individual Indians. The end result of the new system was that many of the Indian hunters-forced-to-turn-farmers were cheated out of their land by greedy whites, and many Indians suddenly found themselves both landless and penniless.

The present-day State of Oklahoma was divided into two governmental divisions and four sections in May of 1890. Indian Territory encompassed all of the eastern one-third of the State and the Cherokee Outlet; Oklahoma Territory included the panhandle, or "No Man's Land," and an area which stretched northeast from the southwestern section to the Kansas border, called "Unassigned Lands," dividing the two sections of Indian land. Further responding to demand for more land for white settlement, additional areas were opened to homesteading in 1891, 1893, 1895, 1901, and 1906. Though some did make illegal homestead claims, the majority of white settlers in the territory of Oklahoma obtained their lands through legal means.

The Oklahoma Land Run of 1889 took place in the Unassigned Lands of present-day Central Oklahoma, and included all or part of modern day Canadian, Cleveland, Kingfisher, Logan, Oklahoma, and Payne counties of the State of Oklahoma. The Unassigned Lands were those lands in present day Central Oklahoma that had not already been assigned to the major Indian tribes by treaties with the US Government. The major tribes (the Choctaw, Chickasaw, Seminole, Cherokee, and Creek) lived on land in Eastern Oklahoma. Members of these tribes were assigned land according to an allotment process based on their registration by the Dawes Commission. Originally, the land they received was not to be sold by the Indians, but in 1909, new legislation was passed that allowed them to sell their Indian allotments. Prior to their registration on the Dawes Rolls, the Creeks lived on the land that had been provided for the tribe by treaty. Because Hoffman was located within the Creek Nation, it was not a direct part of the famous Oklahoma Land Run. Even so, the town and surrounding area were affected by this great event, mostly in terms of how it drew attention to the Indian Territory as a whole.

The great loss of Indian land that resulted from all the changes that took place in the Territory is confirmed by actual figures. In 1873, at the beginning of the reservation policy, the Indian reservations contained about 150 million acres; in 1887, when the Dawes Act was passed, the amount had dropped to 138 million acres; and, eventually, by 1934, when the Dawes Act was repealed, the Indians had only 52 million acres of land.

Not surprisingly, throughout this period a degree of tension always remained just beneath the surface in terms of relations between some Indian groups and whites. Hoffman, for example, was the nearest point to the scene of what was known as the "Snake War," an Indian uprising that took place as late as 1901. Chitto Harjo, or "Crazy Snake," was the leading Indian figure in the uprising, which was created by a disturbance when some army officers raided an Indian camp in search of a stolen saddle. Their abusive tactics provoked enough resentment and anger for the Indians to resort to force to drive them out. Two officers were killed when further troubles followed, and the effect of these events was to create such a state of disturbance and anxiety that the Governor of Oklahoma called out the State Militia. Some of the Indians in Chitto Harjo's tribal faction were placed under arrest.

Since the Indians involved in the uprising belonged to his band, a search of the area was made to locate Harjo. His friends, however, succeeded in hiding him out until the situation quieted down. When there was no further trouble, the Militia was sent home. The affair was played up in the newspapers as a significant Indian uprising and became well known in its time as the "Crazy Snake War." Chief Harjo was rumored to have gone to Mexico, but he had really been hidden on a friend's farm at nearby Smithville. He died there two years later, but, unfortunately, the resentment that existed between some Indians and whites did not die with him.

By 1900 Oklahoma Territory had been expanded to encompass the entire western half of the present-day State and even more, while Indian Territory had been reduced to the eastern section. In June of 1906, Congress provided for the admission of Oklahoma and the Indian Territory to the Union as one State, if both whites and Native Americans approved. Enough support was obtained to gain the necessary approval, and on November 16, 1907, President Theodore Roosevelt proclaimed Oklahoma the forty-sixth State.

MEMBERS OF THE CREEK INDIAN "CRAZY SNAKE" FACTION
UNDER ARREST NEAR HOFFMAN IN 1901
Source: Courtesy of the Archives and Manuscripts Division of the
Oklahoma Historical Society, #3740 and #19367

456

ALLOTMENT DEED.   (40)   CREEK FREEDMAN ROLE ROLL, No. *5301*

THE MUSKOGEE (CREEK) NATION,
INDIAN TERRITORY.

To all whom these Presents shall come, Greeting:

Whereas, By the Act of Congress approved March 1, 1901 (31 Stats., 861), agreement ratified by the Creek Nation May 25, 1901, it was provided that all lands of the Muskogee (Creek) Tribe of Indians, in Indian Territory, except as therein provided, should be allotted among the citizens of said tribe by the United States Commission to the Five Civilized Tribes so as to give to each an equal share of the whole in value, as nearly as may be, and

Whereas, It was provided by said Act of Congress that each citizen shall select, or have selected for him, from his allotment forty acres of land as a homestead for which he shall have a separate deed, and

Whereas, The said Commission to the Five Civilized Tribes has certified that the land hereinafter described has been selected by or on behalf of _____
_____ *George Hawkins* _____, a citizen of said tribe, as an allotment, exclusive of a forty-acre homestead, as aforesaid,

Now, therefore, I, the undersigned, the Principal Chief of the Muskogee (Creek) Nation, by virtue of the power and authority vested in me by the aforesaid Act of the Congress of the United States, have granted and conveyed and by these presents do grant and convey unto the said _____
_____ *George Hawkins* _____, all right, title, and interest of the Muskogee (Creek) Nation and of all other citizens of said Nation in and to the following-described land, viz: *The North East quarter of the South West quarter of Section Four (4), Township Eleven (11) North and Range Twelve (12) East and the West Half of the North East quarter of Section Twenty-nine (29), Township Twelve (12) North and Range Fourteen (14) East.*

SAMPLE LAND ALLOTMENT DEED – PART I
Hoffman Townsite, January 28, 1904

of the Indian Base and Meridian, in Indian Territory, containing ....

.... *One Hundred and Twenty (120)* ....

acres, more or less, as the case may be, according to the United States survey thereof, subject, however, to all provisions of said Act of Congress relating to appraisement and valuation and to the provisions of the Act of Congress approved June 30, 1902 (Public No. 200).

In witness whereof, I, the Principal Chief of the Muskogee (Creek) Nation, have hereunto set

my hand and caused the Great Seal of said Nation to be affixed this .... *28th* ....

day of .... *January* ...., A. D. 190 *4*

.... *P. Porter*

Principal Chief of the Muskogee (Creek) Nation.

DEPARTMENT OF THE INTERIOR,

Approved .... *Feb 29 1904* ...., 190

Ethan A Hitchcock
By Oliver A Phelps   Secretary.
                            Clerk

filed for record on the *7* day of .... *Mar* 1904 , at *4* o'clock *P.* M.

(SEAL)

BUREAU OF INDIAN AFFAIRS
MUSKOGEE, OKLAHOMA
CERTIFIED TRUE COPY

CERTIFYING OFFICER

SAMPLE LAND ALLOTMENT DEED – PART II
Hoffman Townsite, January 28, 1904

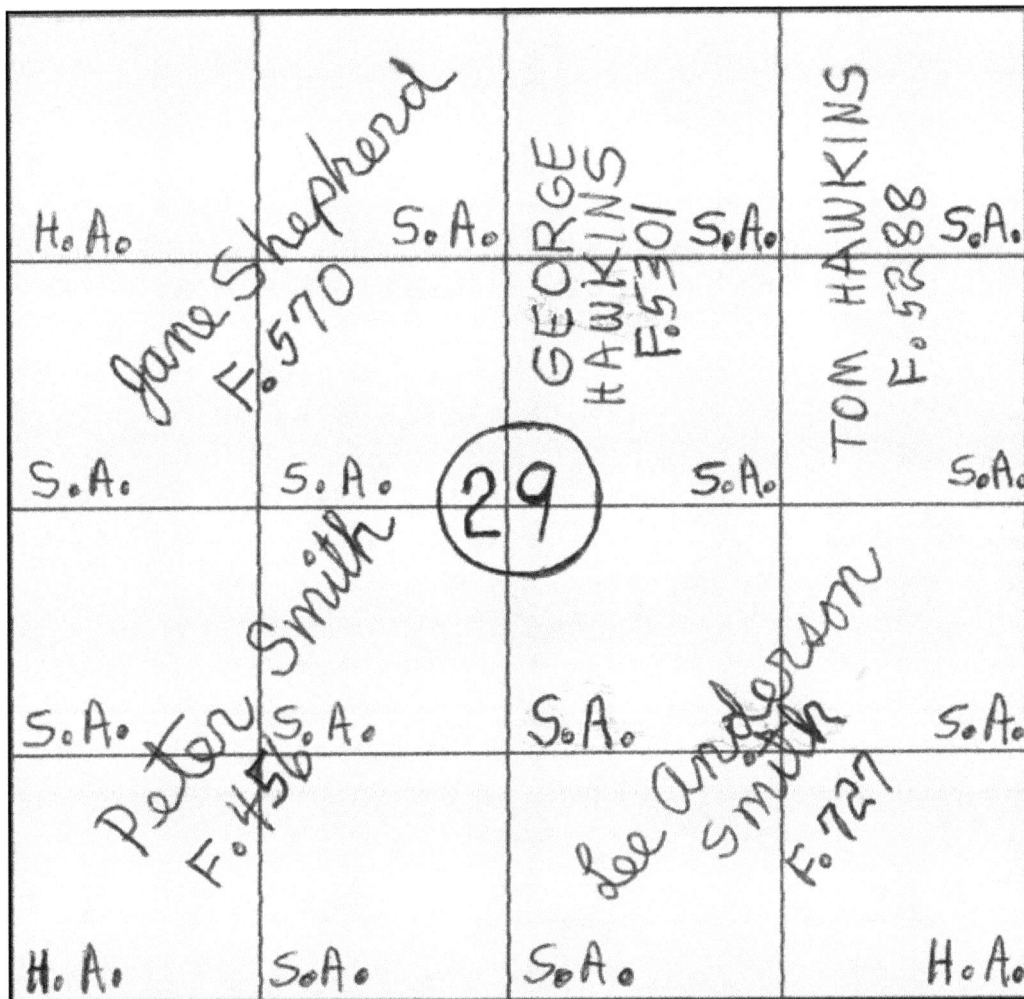

NOTE #1: The large block represents a section of land, or 640 acres. A small block represents 40 acres. "H.A." stands for "Homestead Allotment"; "S.A." stands for "Surplus Allotment." An "F" preceding an allotment role number indicates Chickasaw Freedman rather than a Creek.

NOTE #2: Hoffman was in the Okmulgee Agency of the Bureau of Indian Affairs.

SOURCE: The Bureau of Indian Affairs, Okmulgee, Oklahoma.

CREEK INDIAN LAND ALLOTMENTS AT THE LOCATION THAT LATER BECAME HOFFMAN TOWNSITE

COMPARED ✓

//.............................//.

B 70 P 398 # 22822

........GENERAL WARRANTY DEED RECORD

THIS INDENTURE, Made and entered into this 23 day of August one thousand nine hundred and six by and between David F.Davis , Trustee and of Hoffman I.T. party of the first part and Hoffman Townsite & Realty Company of Hoffman Ind. Ter. party of the second part.

WITNESSETH, That the said party of the first part for and in considera tion of the sum of One & no/1oo Dollars in hand paid, the receipt of which is hereby acknowledged, does hereby grant, bargain, sell, convey and confirm unto the said party of the second part , the following described real estate and premises situate in the Creek Nation, and within the limits of the Indian Territory to-wit: North East Quarter section 29, Township 12 North of Range 14 East

This deed is given to correct former deed given dated June 11, 1906 Recorded in Volume 52, page 478, recorded in U.S.Court at Muskogee Ind. Ter. which former deed was signed as .D.F.Davis Trustee where it should have been signed David F Davis Trustee for Hoffman Townsite & Realty Company. together with all the improvements thereon and the ppurtenances and immunities thereunto belonging or in any wise appertaining., and warrant the title to the same.

~~said sum of mAndy Ido, hereby releasebanddidel inquifhr and in consideration of the~~

And I... wife of the said ..... for and in consideration of said sum of money do hereby release and relinquish unto the said part.. of the second part all my right of ~~dee~~ dower and homestead in and to said lands.

To have and to hold the said lands unto the said party of the second part their heirs, executors, administrators and assigns forever.

IN WITNESS WHEREOF, The said party of the first part has hereunto set his hand and seal the day and year first above written.

Witnesses: As to   David F.Davis   (seal)
                               Trustee for Hoffman Townsite

                    As to   Realty Company   (seal)

SAMPLE LAND TRANSFER RECORD
BY THE HOFFMAN TOWNSITE AND REALTY COMPANY
OF HOFFMAN, OKLAHOMA – PART I

SOURCE: Tract Book E, Pages 432-433, Mcintosh County Courthouse

UNITED STATES OF AMERICA, INDIAN TERRITORY , WESTERN JUDICIAL DISTRICT , S.S.

Be It Remembered, That on this day came before me the undersigned a Notary Public within and for the Western Judicial Disttrict aforesaid, duly commissioned and acting as such David F.Davis to me personally well known as one of theparties grantor in the within and foregoing deed of conveyance and stated that he executed the same for the consideration and purposes therein mentioned and set forth, and I do hereby so certify.

And I do further certify that on this day also voluntarily appeared before me the said ----wife of said ----- to me personally well known to be the person whose name appears upon the within and foregoing deed of conveyance, and in the absence of her said husband declared th t she of her own free will executed said deed and signed and sealed the relinquishmentment of dower and homestead therein expressed for the purposes therein contained and set forth, without compulsion or undueinfluence of her said husband.

WITNESS my hand and seal as such Notary Public on this 24 day of

Aug. 1906   (seal) .(Seal West.Dist)   B.H.Nicholas

MY commission expires jany 17-1907   NotaryPublic

Filed for record this 27 day of Aug. 1906   11 A.M.

                                    R.P.Harrison
                                    Clerk and Ex-Officio Recorder COMPARED
        F   9/1/06

                //........................//

(Continuation)

*SAMPLE LAND TRANSFER RECORD
FOR THE HOFFMAN TOWNSITE AND REALTY COMPANY
OF HOFFMAN, OKLAHOMA – PART II*

*Tract Book E – Pages 432-433
Mcintosh County Courthouse*

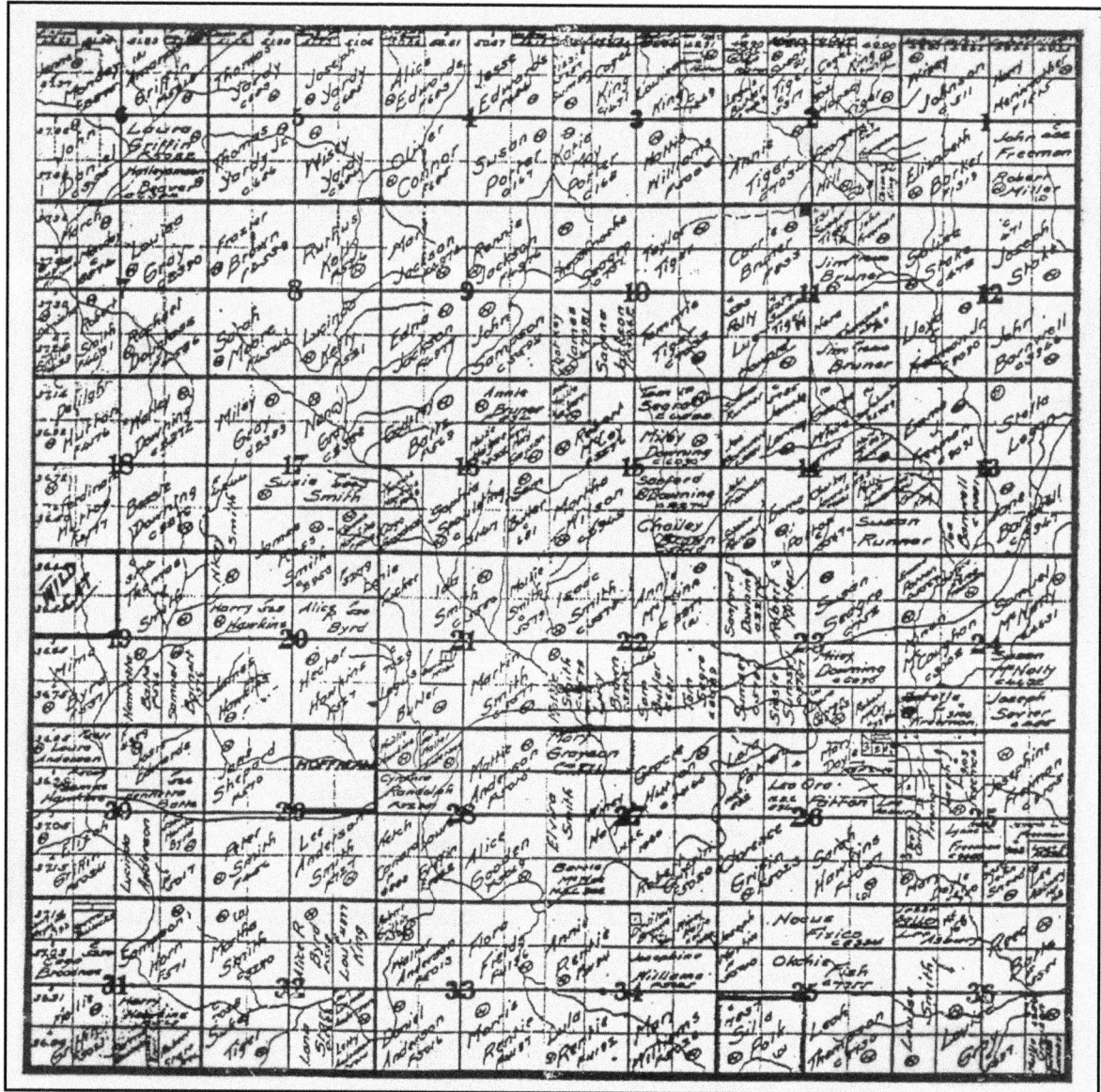

C = Creek Indian; F = Freedman; MC = Minor Creek; MF = Minor Freedman; NBC = New Born Creek; NBF = New Born Freedman; (d) or (D) = Deceased; and H = Homestead.

TOWNSHIP 12 NORTH RANGE 14 EAST
DATE: 1910, PAGE 194-195

Page from Hastain's Township Plats
of the Creek Indian Nation

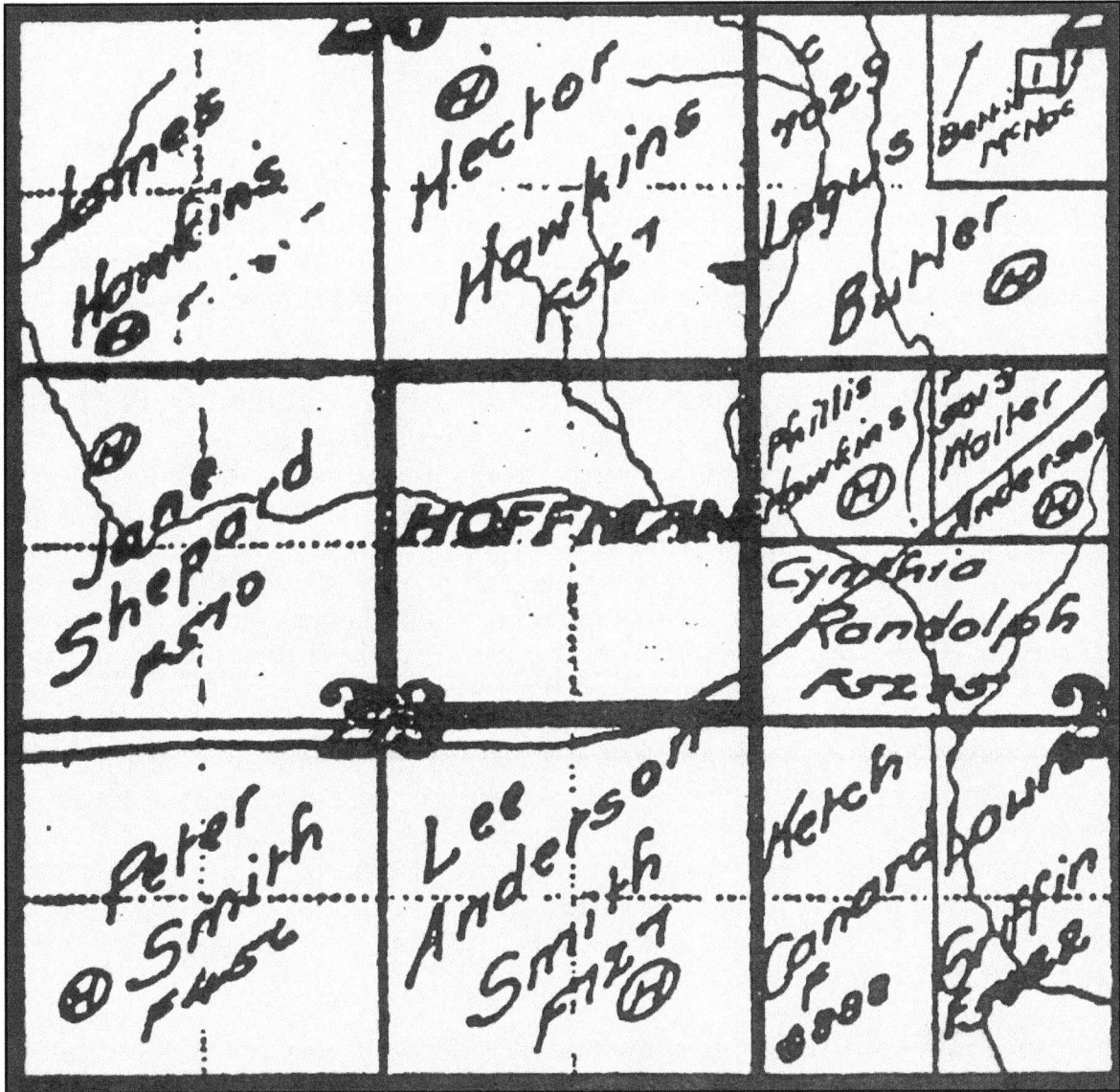

C = Creek Indian; F = Freedman; MC = Minor Creek; MF = Minor Freedman; NBC = New Born Creek; NBF = New Born Freedman; (d) or (D) = Deceased; and H = Homestead.

TOWNSHIP 12 NORTH RANGE 14 EAST
DATE: 1910, PAGE 194

Enlargement of a section of a page from Hastain's Township Plats of the Creek Indian Nation showing the location of The Town of Hoffman

ASSIMILATION
OF THE CREEK INDIANS

Reviewing the lineage of one Creek family in some detail not only helps to visualize what their daily life was like in the early days of Hoffman, but also shows how many if not most of the local Creek Indians are slowly being assimilated into the general population. One good example is the story of the James B. Butler family.

James B. Butler was a full-blood Creek Indian who lived in the Hoffman community. He was born in 1832, probably in Alabama. His heirs recount that in around 1834, he and his parents were forcibly relocated to the Indian Territory in a "Trail of Tears" kind of experience. In later years, he married three full-blood Creek Indian women. With his first wife, Jennie, he had a son who was named Sam. He and his second wife, Dinah Kinha, had two daughters, Martha and Mary. His third wife was Sukey Tiger, and they had one son, Legis. James B. Butler died on March 4, 1883. His gravestone can be seen in the Butler family plot in the Hoffman Cemetery.

James B. Butler's daughter, Martha, whose (nickname was "Matt", lived in or near Hoffman for most of her life. She married a white settler by the name of Jason Perry "Frank" Wilson, who was born in Michigan. (Family and friends in Hoffman always called him Frank.) He moved to Hoffman in the early 1900s to open and operate a livery stable on South Main Street past Broadway Street, out of which he ran a freight hauling business and rented horse-drawn buggies, wagons, and saddle horses.

Frank and Matt Wilson became one of Hoffman's very few affluent families. They owned one home on West Fifth Street and another on land allotted to Martha before her marriage, when all Indians were allotted government land. The farmstead is located one mile north and one and one-half miles east of Hoffman, and today it is still occupied by a member of the family.

Martha "Matt" Butler and Perry "Frank" Wilson had five children: Ada Wilson (born in 1900 and died in infancy), Ida Wilson (1901-1986), Otto Wilson (1905-1906), James B. Wilson (1909-1937), and Otis A. Wilson (1911-1954). Frank and Matt Wilson and their children are buried in the Hoffman Cemetery.

James B. Butler's second daughter, Mary Butler, was born on February 28, 1880. Mary's mother, Dinah Kinha Butler, died when Mary was quite young. She lived with her father and stepmother, Sukie Tiger Butler, for a number of years. In 1895 and 1896, Mary attended the Creek Indian Orphan Asylum in Okmulgee, Oklahoma. Despite its name, this institution was actually a boarding school for Creek Indian children. Upon her enrollment there, the school administrators, believing that Mary should have three names in accordance with white custom, added "Emma" as her first name. From that day forward, she was known as Emma Mary Butler.

On October 4, 1889, Emma Mary Butler married a white settler, as her sister had done. She and her husband, John P. "Pink" Patton, had three daughters, Ora (born 1901), Lora (born 1902), and Dora (born 1905 and died 1912). John Patton died on October 19, 1906. A few years later, Emma Mary married Lee Crisp and had two more daughters, Alma and Marie. On July 1, 1918, Emma Mary died and was buried beside John P. Patton in the Hoffman Cemetery, along with little Dora.

James B. Butler's son, Legis Butler, was born in 1883. He, too, was full-blood Creek, the son of James and Sukey Tiger. It was Legis who sold some of his land to the men who established the Hoffman Cemetery. He complained in later life that he never received all the money the subscribers had pledged to pay for the land. Legis Butler's grave marker is in the Hoffman Cemetery.

The grandchildren and the great-grandchildren of James B. Butler and his wife, Dinah Kinha, lived in Hoffman at one time or another, with a few exceptions. Their granddaughter, Ida Wilson, spent her early years in Hoffman. She married Mack Stow, and they lived for many years on "the old Wilson place," northwest of Hoffman. They had no children.

James B. Butler's grandsons, James B. (Jimmy) and Otis A. Wilson, spent their youth and early adult years in the Hoffman area. Jimmy Wilson never married. Otis A. Wilson and his wife, Billie, had one son, Otis A. Wilson, Jr., who never lived in Hoffman.

Ora Patton, granddaughter of James B. Butler, married Sil Peters, and they had eight children: Nadine, Billye, Cleo, Jim (deceased), Bob (deceased), Jerry, Earl, and Eddy. At the present time, Nadine, Billye, and Eddy live in New Mexico; Cleo and Jerry in California; and Earl in Nevada.

Alma Crisp, another granddaughter of James B. Butler, died at an early age. Her sister, Marie (Maggie) married Earl Mahoney, and they had three children: Patsy, Pete, and Connie. The Mahoneys live in Oklahoma City.

Lora Patton, another granddaughter of James B. Butler, married Marvin Bowden. Their two daughters, Wanda and Joyce, live in New Mexico. As for Ora and Lora, always known as The Patton Sisters, they are truly Hoffman old-timers. As of 1993, Ora (age 92) and Lora (age 91) were enjoying life in Albuquerque, New Mexico. They are proud of their Creek Indian heritage as granddaughters of James B. Butler and Dinah (Kinha) Butler.

Creek Indian full-blood James B. Butler of Hoffman, Oklahoma
Born 1832 - Died March 4, 1883

Mary Butler, daughter of James B. Butler, at the Creek Orphan Asylum
in Okmulgee in 1896. Mary is standing to the left of one of her
instructors, George Riley Hall, with her hands on another
girl's shoulders.

Jason Perry "Frank" and Martha (Butler) Wilson
and Daughter Ida, around 1906

John P. "Pink" and Emma Mary (Butler) Patton
with daughters Lora, Ora and Dora
Hoffman, Oklahoma, 1906

FAMILY GATHERING
AT THE WILSON FARM IN 1907

Pictured (From Left To Right): Seated – Frank Maynard, Frank Bennefield, Jason Perry "Frank" Wilson, (Holding Dean Patton), John Thatcher, and Ross Smith (seated in chair); Standing – Emma Mary (Butler) Patton (Her husband John Patton had recently passed away), Minnie (Patton) Smith (sister-in-law of Emma Mary Patton, who is holding the baby), Fred Smith, three little girls (Ora Patton, Ida Wilson, and Lora Patton), Lem Smith (the boy standing beside his mother's chair), Martha (Butler) Wilson (the woman wearing a white blouse and a dark scarf), and Etta Shepherd; Standing at the end of the porch are Jess Grogan and Bud Smith.
Note #1: Bud Smith was not a son of Ross and Minnie (Patton) Smith; he may have been a relative of Ross's.
Note #2: Names may not be fully accurate.

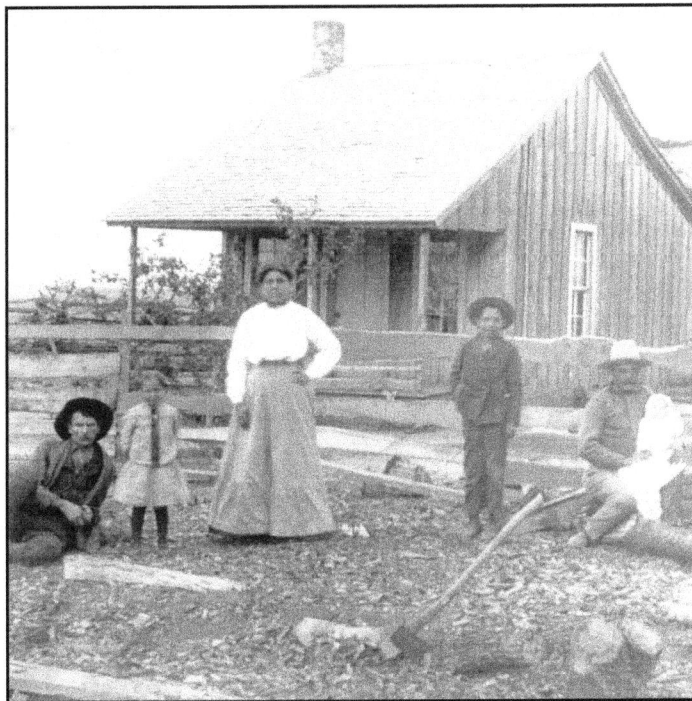

The Wilsons visiting the Smiths, 1907

*Jason Perry "Frank" and Martha (Butler) Wilson and
their daughter Ida at home in the 1910s*

JASON PERRY "FRANK" AND MARTHA (BUTLER) WILSON
WITH SONS OTIS AND JIMMY

NOTE: Frank and Martha were among the first (perhaps the very first) residents of Hoffman to own an automobile.

LINEAL DESCENDENTS OF THE
WILSON BRANCH OF PATRIARCH
JAMES B. BUTLER'S FAMILY

Otis Allen Wilson,
son of Frank and Martha
(Butler) Wilson, during
World War I
(Top Right)

Otis Allen Wilson II,
son of Otis A. Wilson
(Lower Right)

Ty Wilson, son of
Otis Allen Wilson, II
(Bottom Left)

CHAPTER III

BUSINESSES AND PUBLIC SERVICES AT HOFFMAN

INTRODUCTION

Over the years, businesses continued to come and go at Hoffman Townsite, some changing hands often over the years that followed. Some entities lasted for only a brief time, while others continued for decades. Only a sampling of these businesses and their founders and various owners are mentioned in this book. Many changes of ownership are not accounted for, and undoubtedly some of the businesses that are listed are not in correct time sequence. Nevertheless, those that are examined do provide a good overview of the realities of business life at it existed at Hoffman as time passed by. Note that some occupational categories—farm laborers, general laborers and miners, for example—are not separated out in the pages that follow.

Business and accounting practices in those times were not standardized as they are today, and in most of the time there was little or no audit examination of statements by anyone adequately trained in the field. Professional care was not always exercised in business operations, and employees were not always well trained or supervised. Business irregularities and failures were commonplace.

It was not unusual to find business assets and personal assets commingled a situation that made the production of accurate and reliable financial reports almost impossible. The business entity principle of accounting that calls for an enterprise to be accounted for separately and distinctly from the personal affairs of its owner or owners was routinely violated, as was the concept of accounting separately for multiple business entities controlled by the same owner. The reported financial position and net income performance of businesses was often suspect and unreliable.

The principle of objectivity requiring the information in financial statements to be supported by evidence other than someone's imagination or opinion was also routinely violated. With only unreliable and unsubstantiated information backing them, many of the business financial statements that were prepared were often inaccurate and deceiving. Another cause of financial inaccuracy was that reporting was often based on estimates and projections rather than actual costs. Business speculation and boosterism was widespread during the early years of the townsite.

Hoffman got off to a quick start when it first came into being, and early arrivals were enthusiastic and optimistic about their prospects. Unfortunately, from its incorporation as a townsite in 1905 until around 1929, economic conditions there were about as good as they ever got. At one time during the oil boom of the early and mid-1920s, the population of the area jumped to 2,500 people. Many of those who came during this period were temporary residents who left when the oil business took a nosedive due to declining prices in 1926. One of the major non-agricultural employers in the Hoffman area during the early and mid-Twenties was the Kingwood Oil Company.

As those photographs that could be found so plainly indicate, success in any field of business at Hoffman Townsite was in no way something to be taken for granted. The fortunate few who did do well had to earn their success at not only great personal and financial risk--those ever-present blunt realities of small business and entrepreneurship--but also under conditions of significant privation and isolation. Those who were even modestly successful were greatly envied by the majority who were not so lucky. Some of those commercial successes and failures are examined in the pages that follow.

ARRIVAL OF
THE RAILROAD COMPANIES

It was the nearly immediate extension of rail service to the areas made accessible by various Indian Territory land openings that made possible a great boom in the number of homestead claims that were filed and the sudden rise of the petroleum industry a few years later. Oklahoma entered a period of economic growth and prosperity even strong enough to carry it through later declines in the livestock industry and in the value of dry-land farm produce in the years that followed. For many residents of the State, it was the very best of times.

Clearly, local railway service made settlement in areas like Hoffman an economically viable proposition. Without access to rail service, many Oklahoma townsites might never have been developed--or, at the very least, not until many years later than they were. With the active support of the federal government, first the large railroad companies and then regional rail lines created the first economically viable linkage of the Hoffman area with the rest of the country.

In the 1860s and 1870s prior to the coming of the rail lines that were to change the nation, the United States was still a country made up of small farmers who lived off their own land, of independent craftsmen who made one of a kind products in their own workshops, and of small entrepreneurs running their own businesses. Rail access for trade linkage with the rest of the country was indeed crucial to the economic success of the new towns springing up in what was formerly Indian Territory.

Before the availability of rail transportation, the whole country was made up of thousands of little economic islands--communities isolated from each other not only by physical distance but by differing interests. Traveling was difficult, time consuming, and costly. Most people lived in small towns, and they personally knew most of those who lived around them. In fact, most knew everyone in their town by name--not to mention the names of everyone else's spouse, sons, daughters, parents, and grandparents. The world most people occupied back then was not a large place.

By the beginning of the Civil War, the major eastern cities of the United States were already connected by railroad lines. The ride between towns was often uncomfortable and the connections poor, but it was possible to go by train to Boston from New York or from Washington to Philadelphia. It was not possible, however, to go to the west coast by train. Railway maps of the period would have shown a detailed system of railroad tracks in the eastern part of the United States, but from Chicago to the west the map would have been almost totally blank. To get to California or other towns on the Pacific Coast or to send mail there took months of hard travel over mountains and across deserts or a sea trip around Cape Horn.

This situation changed forever when, during the Civil War, the federal government saw the need for a faster way to travel to the western part of the United States to move troops and military supplies. Congress moved to unify the nation by building a railroad system that would cross the entire country. To do so, in 1862 it chartered the construction of two transcontinental railroad lines. The Union Pacific Railroad was to build a track from Omaha, Nebraska, to Utah, while the Central Pacific Railroad was to build a track from Sacramento, California, to Utah.

To help the two rail companies, the federal government subsidized their projects by giving them loans and land grants. Each company was given loans of $16,000 for every mile of track laid on flat land and $48,000 for each mile over mountainous terrain. Public land on both sides of the rail route was divided up in a checkerboard fashion, and the government reserved alternate tracts, each 20 miles square, for the railroad companies' use. In return for this aid, the railroads agreed to transport federal troops and federal mail at reduced rates. When the two lines met in Promontory Point, Utah, on May 10, 1869, the first transcontinental railway had been completed. It now became possible to make a trip across America in the formerly impossible time of one week, a fact that was considered amazing in its day.

The success of the transcontinental railroad projects created a rush of railway construction by other railroad companies. By the 1890s there were four more lines extending from the Midwest to the Pacific Coast, the Southern Pacific, the Northern Pacific, the Great Northern, and the Atchison, Topeka & Santa Fe. These major routes (called "trunk lines"), however, were not the only railroads built during this period. From less than 35,000 total miles of track laid in 1865, the amount increased to 52,000 in 1870, 74,000 by 1875, and 167,000 miles of track in 1890. In the 1880s and 1890s almost 5,000 miles of track were laid every year. The construction included hundreds of feeder lines connecting local towns and cities to major trunk lines.

The federal government's railroad land grant program helped in the building of almost all of these rail lines. The railroads used the land grants not only to build tracks, but also to resell land to settlers and businesses to make money off the westward expansion of the country. In this way the railroads helped to populate the West. They made their land especially attractive to customers, often by offering low fares to people interested in buying western property.

The national railway system completely changed our way of life after the Civil War. By 1890, for example, independent craft workers as a major economic force were gone, their role replaced by unskilled factory workers. The small workshop system was gone as well, replaced by huge industrial plants and mass production. Thousands of independent businessmen were replaced by a much smaller group of powerful industrialists. In the short period of about 20 years, our country became an industrial nation. With the country crisscrossed by railway lines and telegraph wires, the small economic islands that used to exist were effectively linked together into a complex national economy. The only way of life known to most of our people disappeared in this short time period, and permanent changes took place throughout the country.

It was in June of 1904 that these changes first reached the Hoffman area, for it was at that time that Charles W. Raymond, Judge of the United States Court for the Western District, Indian Territory, appointed referees to administer the condemnation and assessment of damages for Indian lands to be used for railroad right of way and other purposes. And it was in August of 1905 that the regional railway company called the Muskogee Union Railway (later to become the Missouri, Oklahoma, and Gulf Railroad Company) built a rail line past the very tract of land that was soon to be selected as the location of Hoffman Townsite. The early residents of the Hoffman area--many of them Indians and freed blacks or their descendants--were immediately affected by this event, just as, in time, of course, everyone in Oklahoma was affected by the growth and expansion of the regional rail system.

A depot for the new railway past Hoffman Townsite was completed on August 15, 1905, and track from the main line to the townsite was finished shortly thereafter. The first train run into Hoffman occurred on August 25, 1905, and the townsite was incorporated in McIntosh County and opened on August 29, 1905.

At one time early in its period of operation, as many as four passenger trains per day ran from the Hoffman Depot of the Missouri, Oklahoma, and Gulf Railroad (nicknamed "Mollie's Old Gal") to the nearest large towns on the line. The trains were loaded not only with local traffic but with people touring the area in search of business prospects. A bus from town was at the depot to meet every train. In later years, a train some called the "Doodlebug" left the depot each morning for the larger nearby town of Henryetta and returned in the afternoon. The MO&G Railroad Company later merged with the Kansas, Oklahoma, and Gulf Railroad Company and became known as the KO&G. The railroad ran from Muskogee, Oklahoma, to Denison, Texas.

Eventually, railroad service to Hoffman Townsite was turned out to be unprofitable, and the spur line was abandoned. The rails were salvaged and reused, but the path of the line can still be seen today. Over the years, many Hoffmanites worked for one or the other of the railroad companies (due to changes of ownership) that provided service to the town. A man by the last name of Patterson, for example, was the roadmaster for many years, and his son, Henry, worked for the railroad as well. For at least part of the 1920s, P. O. Orendorff was the station agent at the Hoffman Depot. One section foreman was named McCarty, and, between 1938-42, Lee Moore was another.

Newly arriving townsite settlers quickly began to build homes, create farms and ranches, open new businesses, provide government services to support local needs, build churches and school buildings, and raise their families with a sense of optimism about their prospects. It should be remembered that the town itself is best thought of, at least initially, as a business. Everyone there was anxious to cash in on the growth and prosperity promised by the townsite's promoters in the then still somewhat exotic area that only a short time before had been exclusively Indian Territory. Coal and oil and commercially harvestable timber had been found in the area, and the air was filled with the expectation of even better times to come.

Only a few of the many individual and family businesses that were active in Hoffman Townsite are photographically profiled in this book, and those that are were selected to provide something approaching a rough cross section of the town's various residents. Some individuals and families that should have been profiled due to the significant role they played in town development are, unfortunately, not covered. In these cases, the omission can be attributed to the simple fact that appropriate photographs of them were not available.

Of the individuals, families and businesses that are mentioned, some were prosperous according to the standards of the times. Most of them, however, were about as "average" as they could possibly be, and some were downright poor and unsuccessful. And because the Creek Indians played such a significant role in the early life of Hoffman Townsite, a special effort has been made to depict that part of Hoffman's heritage. This has been done by profiling in detail one family able to trace its roots back to the times of forced relocation of the Creek Indian tribe to the Hoffman area by federal government action. Many of the town's families could have been profiled to tell a similar story, because many of them had Indian blood on one side of their family or the other.

Many other Hoffmanites are mentioned or pictured in various sections of the book, not because they were in any way remarkable or special but because appropriate photographs were available to illustrate how they lived their lives. Photographs are perhaps the best available means of providing an overview of some of the everyday events and occasions in which people were involved during various periods, thereby making the business and family life of the townsite easier to visualize and to appreciate.

RIGHT OF WAY.

Notice of Condemnation and Assessment of Damages

Isabel Stidham, *Emma Patton* a minor, and mother Amanda Green Cole, Ollie B. Brown, a minor, and father G. C. Brown, Ellen Brown, a minor, Lizzie Thompson, Geo. Carr, Mary Wade deceased, Hettie Hicks, Cornelia Flack. Homer Post, Howard Bailey, a minor and Dr. Tollison stepfather, Jesse Bruner, Spaulding & Hutchison. James Barnett, father of Joe Barnett, deceased, Newman McIntosh, a minor, and Alex McIntosh father, J. D. Hamlin. Benny Bruner, Robison McNac, Emma McNac, Julia McNac deceased, Sol McIntosh, a minor, Millie Derrison, deceased, Polly Derrison, Mary Bray, a minor, W. W. Bray, Della A. Greyson, a minor, Anthony Greyson, Robert Hutchison, Albert McNac, Alex McNac, Myrtie McNac, Amanda Kernells a minor, Temiye Kernells, Annie Kernells Louvina Allen, Willie Hawkins, a minor, M. W. Smith, Samuel McNally, a minor, John T. Wright, Ninon Mc-Coughn, John McCoughn, Miley Downing, Sissie Sumsey deceased, Peter Ewing, "Sumsey" deceased, Albert Tiger, Tom Segro deceased, Chipanoche Seagro, Susan Segro Deere, Sam Butler, deceased, Lucy Brown, Mollie Smith, Martin Smith, Mattie Anderson, Walter Anderson, Phillis Hawkins, Cynthia Randolph, Tom Hawkins, Lee Anderson, Peter Smith, Lucinda Anderson. Henrietta Batts, Thomas Hawkins, and Elijah Griffin, and all other persons interested in the property herein.

You and each of you are hereby notified that the undersigned referees heretofore appointed by the Hon. Chas. W. Raymond, Judge of the United States Court for the Western District, Indian Territory, to determine and appraise the compensation and damages by reason of the condemnation and appropriation of lands hereinafter described to be used by the Muskogee Union Railway for right of way and other railway purposes, will meet at office of United States Commissioners in Court House, Muskogee, Indian Territory, on the 21 day of June, 1904, at ten o'clock a. m., and will then and there proceed with the assessment of damages and compensation for the the appropriation of said lands for the purposes above stated, and will adjourn from time to time until their labors in this behalf are completed, at which time and place, and such other times and places to which the undersigned referees may adjourn, you and all other persons and parties owning or having any interest in or title to the described lands or any part thereof, may appear and be heard.

SW 1-4 Sec. 27 and the S 1-2 Sec. 28, E 1-2 of SE 1-4 Sec. 29 and the SW 1-4 of SE 1-4 Sec. 29, NW 1-4 Sec. 32, W 1-2 and NE 1-4 of NE 1-4 Sec. 31 NW. 1-4 Sec. 31, all in T. 13 N., R. 16 E., and the E 1-2 Sec.36, SW. 1-4 Sec. 36, all in T. 13 N. R. 15 E. NE 1-4 Sec. 2, E. 1-2 of NW 1-4 Sec. 2, and the N 1-2 of SW 1-4 Sec. 3, and the W 1-2, NW 1-4 Sec. 2, and the NW 1-4 Sec. 3.

The SE 1-4 Sec. 3, S 1-2 of SW 1-4 Sec. 3, NE 1-4 Sec. 9, SW 1-4 Sec. 9, S 1-2 Sec. 8, W 1-2 of NW 1-4 Sec. 17, and the N 1-2 of NE 1-4 Sec 18, NW 1-4 Sec. 18, all in T. 12 N., R. 15 E., NE 1-4 Sec 13, NE 1-4 Sec. 24, S. 1-2, NW 1-4 Sec. 24, N 1-2 SE 1-4 Sec. 23, E 1-2, SW 1-4 Sec 23, W 1-2, SW 1-4 Sec 23, SE 1-4 Sec. 22, SW. 1-4 Sec 22, the W 1-2 of SW 1-4 Sec 22, SE 1-4 Sec. 21, NE 1-4 Sec. 28, NW 1-4 of NW 1-4 Sec. 28, NE 1-4 of NW 1-4 Sec. 28, S. 1-2 of NW 1-4 Sec. 28. E 1-2, NE 1-4 Sec. 29, SE 1-4 Sec. 29, SW 1-4 Sec. 29, SE 1-4 Sec. 30, SE 1-4 of NE 1-4 and the S 1-2 of the SW 1-4 of the NE 1-4 Sec. 30, S. 1-2 of NW 1-4 Sec. 30, SW 1-4 Sec. 30, all in T 12 N., R. 14 E. All in the Creek Nation, I. T.

Given under our hand this 3rd day of June, A. D. 1904.

Bert R Greer

W H Jordan

Edward Merrick

Referees.

Sample Land Condemnation Notice
for Railroad Right of Way -- June 4, 1904

*Railroad Construction Crew
near Sapulpa, Oklahoma, in 1905*

*Depot of the Missouri, Oklahoma & Gulf Railroad
at Hoffman, Oklahoma, Around 1914*

Photographs taken on the loading dock (which was referred to as "The Cotton Platform") at the Hoffman Depot of the Kansas, Oklahoma and Gulf Railroad Between 1915 and 1922

Top Left: Ruby Mccoy; Top Right: Kenneth Houston and Minnie Simpson; Bottom: Gathering at the Hoffman Depot in 1916

LAND DEVELOPERS AND
SPECULATORS

Land for Hoffman Townsite was purchased by the Hoffman Townsite and Realty Company, a land development enterprise formed by J. M. Kinyon and G. E. Carney and owned by investors Charles E. Davis, Ira E. Davis, Noah B. Davis, Elmer E. Schock, and J. H. Osborne. The investors purchased the land and formed the townsite for purposes of long-term investment as well as short-term speculation in the form of short-term re-selling before and after the exploitation of natural resources such as timber, oil, and coal. Land acquisition records of the period indicate that some of the developers were careful to buy up mineral rights as well as raw land. The site was located in January of 1905, just in advance of the extension of the original Muskogee Union Railway (again, later called the MO&G Railroad) into the area from Muskogee.

Hoffman Townsite was incorporated in McIntosh County and opened on August 29, 1905. The town was plotted out on 160 acres of freedman land (George Hawkins was the original allottee) that had been put up for resale, drawing interested parties from as far away as Arkansas, Mississippi, Missouri, and other states. The true birthdate of Hoffman was August 29, 1905, the date of sale of the first townsite lot.

Most of the men involved in the townsite development company either already were or were soon to become residents of Hoffman, and they had a vested self-interest in seeing the town grow and prosper. Once in their hands, the land they did not use for personal ventures was immediately marketed as homesite lots for further speculative resale by others. J. M. Carney became the company's land agent--and, later, one of Hoffman's leading citizens--and he immediately began to aggressively promote the townsite to all comers.

Touting the area in glowing terms, it was described in newspaper articles and promotional literature as follows:

Hoffman, I.T., is at present a town of about 500 population, located on the M. O. & G. Railroad about 35 miles southwest of Muskogee and 12 miles east of Henryetta in the center of the Creek Nation, Indian Territory. It is surrounded by the most fertile and productive farm prairie and timber lands in the Territory, which is adapted to all the cereals of the North and also cotton, the king of crops in the South. It is located on a parallel west of Fort Smith, Arkansas, which gives us a climate that has neither extremes of heat or cold. This is demonstrated by the scenic effects produced by the profusion of which all flowers and shrubbery grow, and as a fruit country our soil is unsurpassed.

With these surroundings we have a country we can well feel proud of, and as a location for a town Hoffman has many advantages that will attract the prospective home seeker and speculator, as we have an ideal location for a tile and brick plant and a material that as a clay will stand the inspection of the most skeptical, and we are located accessible to the best coal fields in the Indian Territory. We are also accessible to the Deep Fork of the Canadian River, which would supply any demand for water for manufacturing purposes; and being well timbered with all the harder growths of marketable timber which would supply an unlimited demand for fuel for manufacturing purposes.

Since the time of opening, the town has grown beyond the expectation of all who reside here, and all who visit the place are very agreeably surprised at the marvelous growth of the town and the unsurpassed quality of the soil, that insures the town a good and permanent support. Any desiring a location of any kind or who is looking for a place of investment will receive the most courteous attention by visiting or addressing the Hoffman Townsite & Realty Company.

On April 5, 1905, O. E. O'Bleness, editor of the first newspaper published in Hoffman, the Hoffman Herald, in business from 1905 to 1909, provided a description of Hoffman Townsite, its people, and its buildings.

To begin at the beginning would be somewhat like writing the history before the historian were born, but even this would be possible where the land marks were so plain as they were when the writer of these lines first set his foot on the townsite of where Hoffman now stands. Our first visit to the town was in October of last year, and at that time it consisted only of a few trading places and a very few small dwellings, but after looking over the surrounding country, it took us only a short time to arrive at the conclusion that it was just such as would someday support a thriving city of several thousand people.

Whether it was by accident or otherwise, it matters not, but it is a fact that the townsite people could not have made a better selection for the location of a town than right here where Hoffman now stands. This land is rich, well-watered bottom land and capable of growing a profitable crop of almost anything in the vegetable, fruit or cereal line. To the north of the town lies hundreds, yes, thousands of acres of rolling, black sandy prairie land covered with a growth of bluestem grass from three to five feet high, which is only wanting the attention of the industrious farmer when it will produce crops that will return him a hundred fold for his efforts.

In fact, all the land surrounding the town is rich agricultural land, excepting a range of small hills to the south and west, and they are underlaid with heavy deposits of good coal and vast lakes of oil. In fact, only seven miles west on the M.O.&G. Railway this coal deposit is now being successfully worked and it is only reasonable to presume that at no distant date a profitable coal and oil field will be opened almost within the town limits of Hoffman. Yes, we might go on and write columns regarding the country but the above is sufficient to show that the country around Hoffman when properly farmed is sufficient to support a city of several thousand.

From this point forward, the developers aggressively promoted Hoffman Townsite as an area of great opportunity for homesteaders of all kinds--from those interested in farming and ranching to those interested in forming small businesses or opening professional offices. Interested parties from neighboring states began to make visits to inspect the area, and some stayed on to begin the process of building their own versions of the American Dream. There was no reason at the time to think that the future of Hoffman Townsite would be anything other than promising and bright.

The earliest legal owners of the land that became Hoffman Townsite were the Indian and Indian-adopted former slaves (or their heirs) who had received land allotments from the federal government under programs such as the Dawes Act of 1887. Some of their land had been resold or leased to legal white settlers, and some of it was illegally occupied by squatters and opportunists involved in various kinds of activity. When the first rail line entered the area, land speculators soon arrived on the scene to take advantage of the investment opportunities created by its arrival.

The two lists that follow are in no way exhaustive (and perhaps not totally accurate) of all those who owned land in and around the Hoffman Townsite area, and some who are listed were absentee owners of property who held title for only a short period of time. Some early buyers were interested only in the short-term purchase and resale of land in the hope of making a quick profit. In addition, researchers who have examined land transfer records for the early years of the townsite development period have found that some white trustees appointed by the courts to "help" the Indian and Negro land allottees actually either bought the land from them for a pittance or defrauded them of its true value through other legal but highly unethical means.

According to a referee's notice from June 3, 1904, some of the landowners mentioned in a federal court land condemnation action for railroad right-of-way access into the Hoffman area were as follows: Emma Patton, Isabel Stidham, a minor, and her mother Amanda Green Cole, Ollie B. Brown, a minor, and his father G. C. Brown, Ellen Brown, a minor, Lizzie Thompson, George Carr, Mary Wade (deceased), Hettie Hicks, Cornelia Flack, Homer Post, Howard Bailey, a minor, and his stepfather Dr. Tollison, Jessee Bruner, Spaulding & Hutchison, James Barnett, father of Joe Barnett (deceased), Newman McIntosh, a minor, and his father Alex McIntosh, J. D. Hamlin, Benny Bruner, Robison McNac, Emma McNac, Julia McNac (deceased), Sol McIntosh, a minor, Millie Derrison,(deceased), Polly Derrison, Mary Bray, a minor, W. W. Bray, Delia A. Greyson, a minor, Anthony Greyson, Robert Hutchison, Albert NcNac, Alex McNac, Myrtle McNac, Amanda Kernells, a minor, Temiye Kernells, Annie Kernells, Louvina Allen, Willie Hawkins, a minor, M. W. Smith, Samuel McNally, a minor, John T. Wright, Ninon

McCoughn, John McCoughn, Miley Downing, Sissie Sumsey, deceased, Peter Ewing, "Sumsey," deceased, Albert Tiger, Tom Segro, deceased, Chipanoche Seagro, Susan Segro Deere, Sam Butler, deceased, Lucy Brown, Mollie Smith, Martin Smith, Mattie Anderson, Walter Anderson, Phillis Hawkins, Cynthia Randolph, Tom Hawkins, Lee Anderson, Peter Smith, Lucinda Anderson, Henrietta Batts, Thomas Hawkins, and Elijah Griffin.

Ownership records on file in the McIntosh County Courthouse show that some additional early owners of Hoffman Townsite land were the following: M. O. Smith, J. N. Womack (or Warmack), Osee and Emma Nelson, James H. Bruton, F. M. Cash, Benjamin Cash, B. Coward, Mrs. Doyle Maud, Maud and Doyle Wallace, B. F. and Ida Coward, L. Johnson, A. Vinenson (and some partners), the Farmers and Merchants Bank, Sanders Greenberry, W. L. Smith, T. J. Barr, T. A. Fleshman, Dan Barr, Lorena May Pearlen, Madeline A. Lee, W. H. Lillian, J. R. Richardson, Elizae Brewer, W. W. Dilley, Thomas D. Smith, George E. Carney, Joseph D. Black, David F. Davis, L. A. Chatham, the Home Mission Building, Dora D. Smith, Harry and Stella Ritterhoff, and J. A. Osborne.

BANKING COMPANIES AND FINANCIERS

The first permanent business building ever erected at Hoffman Townsite was the home of the First Bank of Hoffman. One member of the Davis family, D. E. Davis, became its first president while another, Ira E. Davis, became its vice president. Yet another member of the family, Noah B. Davis, became its cashier. The bank opened for business on August 12, 1905, with $11,000 in capital stock. Patrons were said to be so satisfied with its service that by as early as late 1905 the owners were contemplating the construction of a new two-story brick building. The Davis brothers, like many other early townsite residents, also bought up many of the township lots as speculative properties.

A second bank in town, owned by D. W. Kinsey and Ed Carney, was the Farmers' and Merchants' Bank, or, simply, the Farmers' Bank. It, too, was capitalized at $11,000. The president of the Farmers' bank was J. W. Brown, the vice president was G. E. Kearney, and the cashier was D. W. Kinsey. Like the owners of the other bank in town, these owners also engaged in land speculation on their own right. Yet another banker was Meyer's Bank, but nothing about it (other than the name) could be found.

Banking and investment companies were almost totally unregulated in those times. With little or no oversight or operating guidelines to restrict their activities, the public was not well protected from poor business practices, fraud and embezzlement, or overt criminal activity. Again, the owners of the local banks freely speculated on local properties and business ventures on their own right. In addition, personal assets had a way of becoming commingled with the assets of their banks. In the absence of any effective regulation or oversight, the wonder is that there were not even more problems than there were.

The First Bank of Hoffman and
The Hoffman Townsite and Realty Company, Inc.

SOME LEADING FIGURES IN THE
EARLY DEVELOPMENT OF HOFFMAN TOWNSITE

Top Left: Dr. Charles E. Davis, Real Estate Investor; Top Right: J. M. Howk, President – K. H. & Company Real Estate; Bottom Left: Noah B. Davis, Investor and Cashier, First Bank of Hoffman; Bottom Right: J. M. Kinyon, Sole Agent -- Hoffman Townsite and Realty Company, Inc., and General Manager of K. H. & Company Real Estate

NOTICE OF INCORPORATION, HOFFMAN.

Notice is hereby given that on April 13th, 1906, there was filed in the clerk's office for the United States Court for the Western District of the Indian Territory at Muskogee, a petition of the inhabitants of the town of Hoffman, Indian Territory, for the incorporation of said town.

That said petition is signed by more than twenty qualified voters, inhabitants of said town, embracing the described lands situated the Creek Indian, Indian Territory, Western Judicial District thereof as follows, to-whit--

Beginning at the Southeast corner of the Northwest quarter of Section Twenty-nine (29) of Township Twelve (12) North, and Range Fourteen (14) East; Thence South two hundred and fifty (250) feet; Thence West to a point directly South of the Southwest corner of Block Forty-seven (47) in said town of Hoffman; Thence North to the Northwest corner of Block Fifty-five (55); Thence East to the Northeast corner of Block Seven (7); Thence South to the place of beginning.

That annexed to said petition is an accurate map or plat of the lands proposed to be incorporated with the incorporate limits of said town.

That the name proposed for said town is Hoffman.

That the inhabitants of said town have appointed J. M. Kinyon, G. EDD. Carney and E. L. Shults as their agents.

That the Honorable William R. Lawrence, Judge of the United States Court for the Western District of the Indian Territory on Saturday, April 14th, 1906, on the presentation of said petition in open Court, ordered that the hearing of said petition for incorporation be set for Thursday, May the 24th, 1906, at Nine o'clock a. m. of said day and date.

This 20th day of April, 1906.
   J. M. Kinyon,
   G. EDD. Carney, } Agents
   E. L. Shults.

[First Publication April 26th, 1906.]

Free Transportation.

From all points on the M. O. & G. railway to Hoffman and return. All parties wishing to purchase property in Hoffman will be given free transportatiOn if upon the purchase of your ticket you will ask the agent for receipt for the same. Upon the, presentation of said receipt and voucher from the Hoffman Townsite & Realty Co; showing you have purchased property in the town of Hoffman your money so paid wlll be refunded by the M. O. & G. Railroad Co;

HOFFMAN TOWNSITE& REALTY CO.
Approved by W. P. Dewar,
Vice Pres. M. O. & G. R'y.

Any ticket agent, on the M. O. & G. R. R. will sell you a ticket, to Hoffman I. T. and give you a receipt for the purchase price of same, and K. H. & Co. will return the amount to you if you buy a Farm or lease from them.

J. M. Kinyon Mgr.

M. O. & G. Time Card.
EAST
No. 4, Passenger, ... 3:30 p.m.
No. 34, Local freight, ...8:55 a.m.
WEST
No. 1, Passenger, ... 11:30 a.m.
No. 31, Local, ... 4:45 p.m.

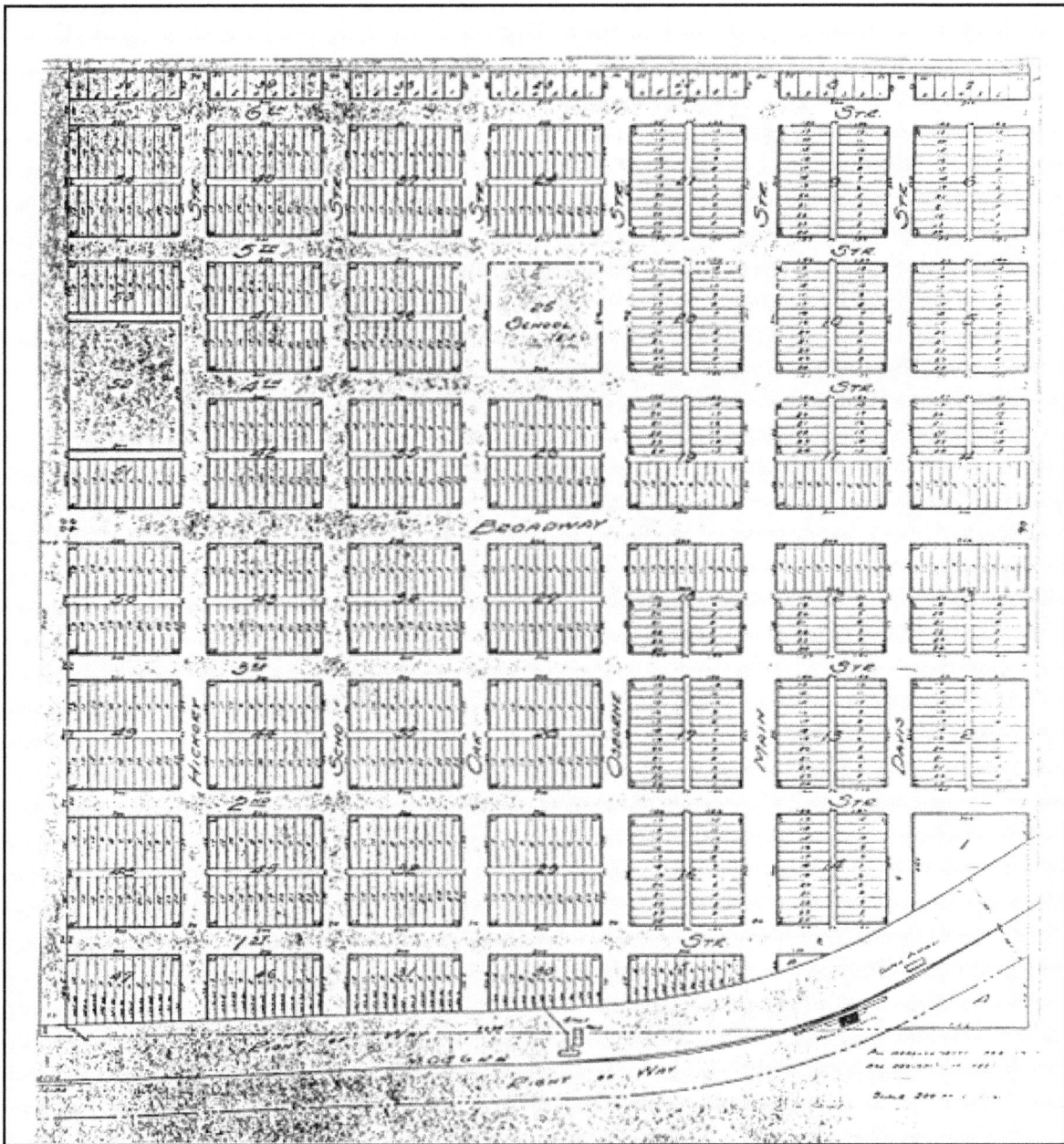

ORIGINAL HOFFMAN TOWNSITE PLAT MAP
Filed on August 21, 1905, in the Indian Territory

*Hoffman in 1906, looking north from the corner
of Main and Broadway. Note the row of businesses
on both sides of Main Street*

*Irving Vanderpool looking west from atop a low hill outside
of Hoffman, an eastward view of the town behind him*

Settlers arriving on their land at Hoffman townsite by covered wagon, around 1910. Pictured are Joe and Maudina "Exie" Kersey and daughter Violet, who later married Joe Burney and became a lifelong Hoffmanite.

Pierce, Mitt, Street, Fisher, Joe and Molly Burney (seated), around 1920. The family moved to Hoffman from North Carolina. (Names are incomplete and may be out of order.)

Top Left: George Jackson and Virginia Victoria (McFarlin) Martin, around 1900. Top Right: Brothers Delmar and Mack Parker, Early Residents of Hoffman. Bottom Left: Charlie E. Lackey, another early resident of Hoffman. Bottom Right: George Martin (Top), Unknown (Left) and Dick Martin, who moved from Arkansas to Hoffman.

HOFFMAN, OKLAHOMA, AROUND 1900

STREET MAP OF HOFFMAN AS IT WAS FROM 1911 TO 1918
Hand-drawn from memory by former resident
Lora (Patton) (Bowden) Jennings

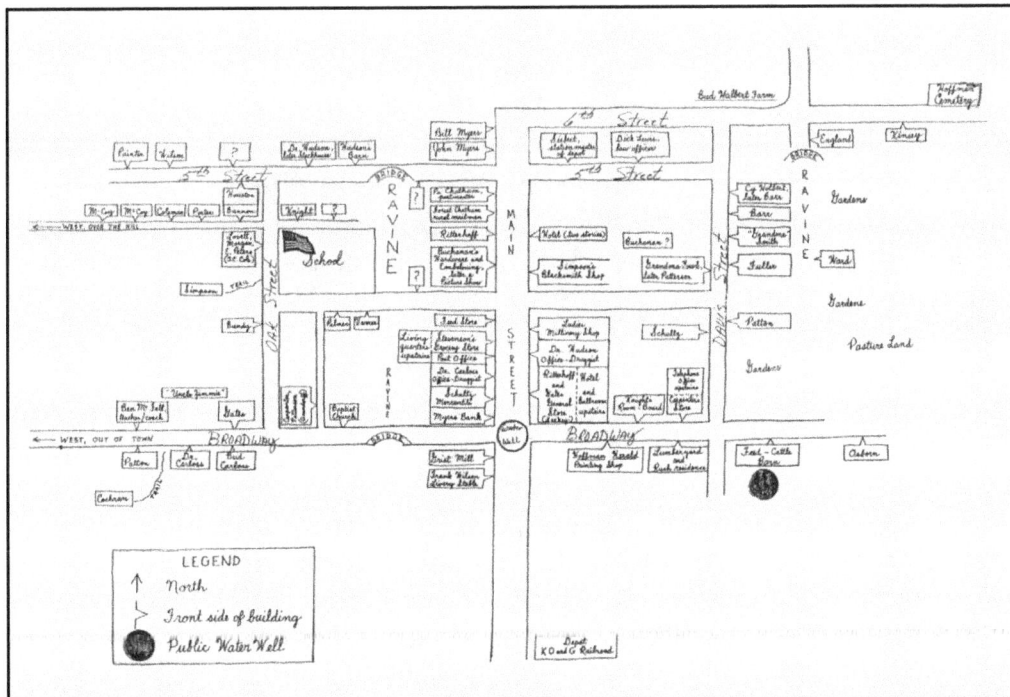

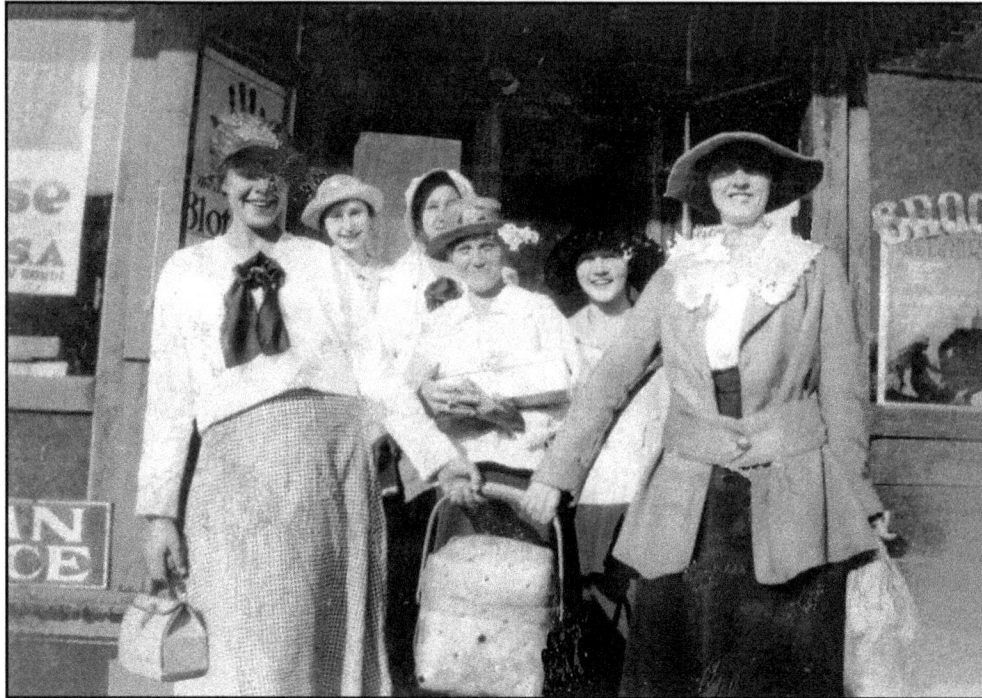

*Ladies picnic shopping at a grocery store in Hoffman
on October 23, 1918, during World War I*

POSTAL SERVICE, NEWSPAPERS AND
PUBLIC SERVICES

The first post office in Hoffman was established on December 18, 1905. It stayed on the list of McIntosh County post offices until April 10, 1922, when it was discontinued. It was then listed in Okmulgee County from April 11, 1922, to September 20, 1985, when it was again discontinued. The post office building was once located on the east side of Main Street and once on the west side of Main Street, and it may have been situated in other places as well. In even later years, it was located in the front of a private home. Since 1985, mail for Hoffman has been routed through the Henryetta post office.

Over the years, a number of different men brought the daily mail from the railroad depot to the post office or handled mail delivery service. In the very early days of the town, this was done with a horse and wagon. Among those who carried mail from the depot to town were a black man by the name of George Anderson and another man by the name of Mack Parker. Among those who served as rural mail carriers were P. L. Orendorff, Mr. Caviness, and Burl Larimore. A partial listing of the town's postal service staff and postmasters appears in the table that follows.

The first newspaper was available in Hoffman even before the town was incorporated as a townsite. The Hoffman Herald was published from April 5, 1905, through October 14, 1909, when it closed down. It was not replaced until 1915, when the Hoffman Observer, a paper that lasted only a few months--from March through May of 1915--came to town. Both papers (especially the early one) were essentially captive mouthpieces of the developers, speculators and financiers who were intent on making money off the Indian Territory Land Rush.

It was the editor of the first newspaper, O. E. O'Bleness, known as a staunch Republican, who provided detailed descriptions of some the early business buildings, residences, and the growth of Hoffman, along with profiles of some of leading businessmen during the early days of the town that appear in this book. Editor O'Bleness was an early investor and avid promotor of the townsite. He was also very much involved in the civic and religious activities of the community.

On October 15, 1906, while Hoffman Townsite was still part of Indian Territory, a group of "country" men joined together to form a joint stock company for the purpose of buying a site for a public cemetery. A short time later, a group of "town" men donated money to fence in the cemetery site that was to be purchased. The result of their effort was the Hoffman Public Cemetery, which was located on the north edge of town. Oklahoma did not become a state until one year later. A record of the land purchase and fencing agreements that occurred back then appears on the pages that follow. The cemetery is still in use today.

Land for the cemetery was sold to the founders by Legis Butler, a full-blood Creek Indian who was a resident of Hoffman. Legis, by the way, complained in later years that he never received all the money the cemetery founders had pledged to him for giving up his land.

Public-spirited citizens actively participated in various town-building activities and subscription projects. A town government was established, and levies and fees of several kinds were approved to cover the costs of street improvement, bridge construction, school construction, police and fire protection, and so on. On other occasions, able-bodied citizens were expected to donate time for civic projects designed to promote the common good. Townsite organization and development seemed to move along very nicely during these early days.

Space not occupied by business concerns in what was called the Hoffman House Business Building was used as a public hall and lodge room. Lodge 211 of the I.O.O.F. was active in Hoffman at the time. Early civic business was conducted at this location.

The Pioneer Telephone Company (replaced in 1907 by the Council Hill Telephone Company) reached town by 1906. At least until between 1938-1942, there was still a telephone office in Hoffman. It was clerked during those years by Louise (Hamilton) Nicholson, Josie Hamilton, and Grace (Fuller) Robinson.

Hoffman also supported a volunteer fire department, two public schools (one for whites and one for blacks), and a jail and a sheriff. At one time, Jim Rose served as sheriff and Tom Knight served as his deputy. Almost up to the 1940s, both men wore handguns slung on the hip in the old west style.

HOFFMAN POST OFFICE
OKMULGEE COUNTY, OKLAHOMA

APPOINTED	STAFFING	TITLE
12-18-05	Edwin L. Shultz	Postmaster

Originally established in the Creek Nation, I.T.

10-24-07	William L. Smith	Postmaster

Changed to McIntosh County, Oklahoma, in 1907

11-11-13	Lemuel A. Chatham	Postmaster

Changed to Okmulgee County of April 11, 1922

09-20-32	Mrs. LeVeta M. Lewis	Acting Postmaster
02-01-33	Mrs. Dorothy L. Harriman	Postmaster
04-16-43	Miss Helena M. Hood	Acting Postmaster
04-15-44	Miss Helena M. Hood*	Postmaster

*Name changed by marriage on June 27, 1946,
to Mrs. Helena M. Chadwick*

08-24-53	Mrs. Georgia E. Duvall	Acting Postmaster
09-30-54	Mrs. LeVeta M. (England) Lewis	Acting Postmaster
06-30-55	Mrs. LeVeta M. (England) Lewis	Postmaster
06-11-82	Brenda D. Britt	Officer-in-Charge
11-10-82	Service Suspended	
09-20-85	Service Discontinued; Mail via Henryetta	

No. H
(LOCATION PAPER.)

No. 1841.

Post Office Department,

OFFICE OF THE FOURTH ASSISTANT POSTMASTER GENERAL,

DIVISION OF APPOINTMENTS.

WASHINGTON, D. C., ..., 190 .

SIR: Before the Postmaster General decides upon the application for the establishment of a post office at ...., County of ...., State of ...., it will be necessary for you to carefully answer the subjoined questions, get a neighboring postmaster to certify to the correctness of the answers, and return the location paper to the Department, addressed to me.

If the site selected for the proposed office be not on any mail route, only a "Special Office" can be established, to be supplied with mail from some convenient point on the nearest mail route by a special carrier, for which service a sum equal two-thirds the salary of the postmaster will be paid by the Department.

You should inform the contractor, or person performing service for him, of this application, and require him to execute the appended certificate as to the practicability of supplying the proposed office with mail.

Very respectfully,

P. W. Graw

Fourth Assistant Postmaster General.

To Mr. ....

care of the Postmaster of ...., who will please forward to him.

STATEMENT.

The proposed office to be called *Hoffman, District 10.*

⚜ **Notice directions for selecting post office names on next page.** ⚜

It will be situated in the *N.E.* quarter of Section *2 9*, Township *12*, (North and south). Range *14* (East and west), in the County of *Creek Nation*, State of *Indian Territory*.

It will be on or near route No. .... being the route from *Morris* to *Grayson* on which the mail is now carried *six* times per week.

Will it be directly on this route?—Ans. *No.*

If not, how much would its supply on this route increase the distance necessarily traveled by the carrier in going once over the route? *2 mile*

If not on any route and a "Special Office" is wanted, from what office to be supplied? *Grayson*

The name of the nearest office to the proposed one, on one side, is *Grayson.*

Its distance is *2* miles in a *N.W.* direction from the proposed office.

The name of the nearest office, on the other side, is *Boynay*

Its distance is *5* miles in a *S.W.* direction from the proposed office.

The name of the other nearest office to the proposed one is *Fuyrtta*

Its distance by the most direct road is *13½* miles in a *S.W.* direction from the proposed office.

The name of the most prominent river near it is *Deep Fork of the Canadian*

The name of the nearest creek is ....

The proposed office will be *1½* miles from said river, on the *north* side of it, and will be .... miles from said nearest creek, on the .... side of it.

The name of the nearest railroad is *the M.O.+G. Ry.*

If on the line of or near a railroad on which side will the office be located; how far from the track; and what is, or will be, the name of the station?—Ans. North side, 50 Rds from depot named Hoffman

Give the population to be supplied by the proposed office.—Ans. 2,000

If it be a village, state the number of inhabitants.—Ans. this town 250 at present

A diagram, or sketch from a map, showing the position of the proposed new office, with neighboring river or creek, roads, and other post offices, towns, or villages near it, will be useful, and is therefore desired.

ALL WHICH I CERTIFY to be correct and true, according to the best of my knowledge and belief, this 15th day of August, 190 5

[☞ Sign full name.] Edwin L. Shuler Proposed P. M.

I certify that I have examined the foregoing statement, and that it is correct and true, to the best of my knowledge and belief.

(This must be signed by Postmaster at nearest office.)

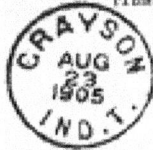

Samuel J. Smith
Postmaster at Grayson Ind Ter.

[OVER.]

*At a "special office" the postmaster is sum not exceeding two-thirds of the postal

tions of the citizens interested

Diagram showing the site of the _Hoffman_ Post Office, in Township _12_ (N. or **X**), Range _14_ (E. or **X**) of _Indian Base_ Meridian, County of _Creek Nation_ of _Indian Territory_, with the adjacent Townships and Post Offices.

It is requested that the exact site of the proposed or existing Post Office, as also the roads, the adjoining offices, and the larger streams or rivers, be marked on this diagram, to be returned as soon as possible to the Post Office Department.

Range 13. E.   Range 14. E. (NORTH.)   Range 15. E.

Okmulgee ⊗

Town 13, N   Town 13, N

Town 12, N   Town 12, N

6—5—4—3—2—1
7—8—9—10—11—12
16—17—16—15—14—13
19—20—21—22—23—24
30—29—28—27—26—25
31—32—33—34—35—36

Town 11, N   Beggs   Town 11, N

Scale one-third inch to the mile.   (SOUTH.)

INSTRUCTIONS RELATIVE TO NAMES OF POST OFFICES.

Attention is called to the following order issued by the Postmaster General, dated **April 9, 1894**:

"ORDERED, No. 114.—To remove a cause of annoyance to the Department and injury to the Postal Service in the selection of names for newly established post offices, it is hereby ordered, that from this date only short names or names of one word will be accepted. There may be exceptions when the name selected is historical, or has become local by long usage, but the Department reserves the right in such cases to make the exception or not as it sees proper. Names of post offices will only be changed for reasons satisfactory to the Department."

The prefix of "East," "Old," "New," "North," "South," or "West," to the name of a post office is objectionable; as also is the addition of "Burg," "Center," "City," "Corners," "Creek," "Cross Roads," "Depot," "Hill," "Hotel," "Hollow," "Junction," "Mill," "Mound," "Peak," "Plains," "Point," "Port," "Prairie," "Rock," "River," "Run," "Ridge," "Store," "Station," "Springs," "Town," "Vale," "Valley," or "Village," and all other prefixes or additions, as such prefixes or additions are liable to lead to confusion and delay in transmission of the mails.

Delay may often be avoided by here submitting in order of preference several names as the one first selected may be rejected by the Department.

ESTABLISHMENT OF POSTAL SERVICE
AT HOFFMAN -- PAGE 3 OF 3

Hoffman Ind, Ter. October, 15th, 1906.

We the undersigned Citizens, of Hoffman I.T. agree to pay the amount set opposite our respective names, for the porpose of buying a cemetary ci te for a joint stock Company.

NAMES	AMOUNT	
Andrew Armstrong Sr	$30.00	Paid
Jason Wilson	5.00	X
J. B. Bernefield	5.00	
Henry Phillip	2.50	
J. D. Tidwell	2.50	X
E. J. Gray	1.00	X
B. B. Bray	1.00	X
Isaac Smith	5.00	X
L. B. Wilson	1.00	X
W. B. Bramfield		
W. R. Middleton	2.50	X
Edwards	1.00	
B. S. Blankenship	$5.00	X
J. F. Edwards	$5.00	X
J. M. Edwards	5.00	
J. W. Edwards	5.00	
D. L. Maxwell	1.00	X
A. R. Edwards	5.00	
J. B. A	1.00	X
James R Smith	5.00	
L. B. Grogan	2.50	
Otis Shouldeny	6.00	X
Jack Quinton	1.00	X
Thos. M. Smith	2.50	X

Fund raising appeal for a public cemetery at Hoffman
October 15, 1906

*Legis and Rhonda Butler, Creek Indian couple who sold land
for a public cemetery in Hoffman*

Our New Cemetery.

The country people went to work this week and cleared off the cemetery cite and made a proposition that they would also put up the fence if the town people would furnish the material. A petition was circulated and in about two hours time the necessary funds were raised. The following named donated.

Frank Carpenter,	$ 2.00
O. E. O'Bleness,	2.00
D. W. Kinsey,	5.00
G. E. Carney,	2.00
L. A. Chatham,	2.00
H. J. Kinyon,	1.00
L. E. Davis,	2.00
F. C. Chatham,	1.00
T. C. Carlosa,	1.00
Harry Ritterhoff,	1.00
T. W. Carpenter,	2.00
E. L. Shults,	2.00
R. L. Lewis,	1.00
D. N. Kelker,	2.00
J. H. Breeding,	.50
W. G. Julian,	.50
C. B. Herman,	1.00
W. W. Buchanan,	1.00
J. S. Carter,	1.00
G. J. Stevenson,	.50
Wm. England,	.50
E. L. Owens,	1.00
O. C. Nelson,	1.00
B. B. and C. A. Halbert	1.00
E. B. Wright,	.50
John West & Son,	2.00
R. O. Easley,	1.00
Jas. Bannan,	1.00
J. H. Rice,	1.00
R. T. Ford,	.25
F. M. Hall,	1.00
J. S. Boling,	.25
W. H. Hays,	.50
F. M. Gash,	1.00
W. L. Varner,	.50
Dr. Harris,	1.50
Bill Knight,	.25
J. N. Shults,	2.00
J. W. Cape,	1.00
S. P. Middleton,	1.00
O. F. Wiseman,	.50
J. C. Snelson,	.50
J. D. McReynolds,	.25
H. Knight.	.50
J. O. Snelson,	.50
Brown Lumber Co.,	5.00
Sears & Roebuck,	00.00
Montgomery, Ward & Co.,	00.00
Kemper-Paxton Merc. Co.,	00.00
Total,	$ 56.00

Establishment of a public cemetery
at Hoffman in 1906

Along in the early part of February the people of Hoffman began to agitate the question of building a bridge across the Deep Fork at a point one mile south of town, so that the large number of settlers living on the south side within our trade territory could do their trading here instead of going elsewhere which they have had to do a greater part of the time heretofore. As an illustration of the manner in which they do things down in Indian Territory we will say that the matter was taken up in February, since which time the necessay funds have been raised by popular subscription, bridge built and paid for; and by Saturday of next week will be ready to accomodate any and all who may want to come to do their trading in the best town in the Creek Nation. The structure cost in round numbers $550.00 and it's all paid for without a dollars' worth of taxes or bonds being voted for the home seeker to help pay, who desires to cast his lot among us.

Fund raising campaign for a bridge over the Deep Fork River

*The old swinging bridge over the Deep Fork River
at Hoffman in 1914*

*Nellie Peters, Kenneth Houston and Ruby Mccoy on the
old swinging bridge across the Deep Fork River outside of Hoffman*

On the old swinging bridge over the Deep Fork River
Pictured are Sibyl Ferguson (left), Kathleen Orendorff
(center), and Vara Ferguson

Hoffman to Get Gas Supply

To Be Piped Into Town Soon---Now Let's Get Electricity For Lights and Power.

In the not far distant future Hoffman will be up-to date with other towns as there is a move on foot now to pipe gas into the town and to the various parts of town. This is a laudable move and the people of Hoffman will receive the modern improvement with much delight. Now, that gas is a certainty let's turn our attention toward electricity for power and lighting purposes. With this improvement will come a good moving picture show and give the people a place of amusement. It takes all these things to make a live town and the cost is only a trifle. Make Hoffman bigger and better.

Establishment of natural gas service
at Hoffman -- April, 1915

PUBLIC SCHOOLING

Critical to the success of the new towns started in Indian Territory in the early 1900s was access to schooling for the children of the people enticed to settle in them. Hoffman's promoters and civic leaders played an active part in starting a school and in making sure that it prospered. In the very early days even before the townsite had drawn in many white settlers there was a government school in the area, probably one that served only the Indian population.

By as early as April of 1906, however, 35 of the town's 50 eligible children had been enrolled in what was called the "Hoffman Free School." The school administrator at the time was Captain W. A. Bradshaw, whose fundamental rule of school administration was "Do right!" School funding was initially obtained by levees against the users of the facility. On January 17, 1907, for example, school trustees D. N. Keller, I. E. Davis, and L. A. Chatham levied an assessment of $.50 per month on each child against patrons for operating funds and staff salaries.

From 1905 until 1918, Hoffman School was part of the McIntosh County Public School District. When the town became part of Okmulgee County in 1918, jurisdiction passed to the Okmulgee County School District. All grade levels of white students (until integration in the 1960s) attended Hoffman School on the north side of town; black grade school students attended a "colored separate" school on the south side of town and high school students attended school in nearby Grayson. The last "colored" grade school site was south of town near the old railroad line and a block to the west of Main Street. (It may have been in a church.) In later years, all grade levels of black students attended nearby Grayson School, until it, too, was closed in the 1960s. Interestingly, the last buildings used as grades schools for white and colored students are both still in use, today as churches.

For more information about Hoffman School, read *"My Indian Territory School"* and *"A Photographic History of Hoffman School in Okmulgee County, Oklahoma."* Both books delve into its story, supplementing it with scores of photographs.

A Free School for Hoffman.

Capt. Bradshaw, a member of the National Creek School Department arrived in Hoffman Sunday and at once began to arrange for the organization of a special school district and the institution of a government school. Monday night he met with the school board chosen by the Commercial Club and together they perfected a permanent organization and defined the contingent lines of said district. Capt. Bradshaw subsidized the government school to our Board of Education and declared it his intention to operate in harmnory with them. He met the children in the Carney Hall Tuesday and made a list of books to be furnished by his department. The new school building will be completed and school opened there Monday morning. this is undoubtedly a great thing for our town as it furnishes a teacher for the entire scholastic year from now until statehood time, at $45.00 per month. Capt. Bradshaw is a young man of considerable experience and fair education and under his direction our school will be placed on a firm foundation. He will remain with us until June at least.

Money to Loan.

We will loan money of any reasonable amount, at low rates on good agricultural lands.

W. A. BRADSHAW, MGR.,
Hoffman, I. T.

School Notes.

✦ ✦ ✦ ✦

Enrollment this week in the Hoffman free school, 35.

Mr. Bradshaw's fundamental rule for the school goverment is: 'Do Right'.

A choir was organized in shool this week with Miss Minnie Kelker as leader and organist.

Capt. Bradshaw has offered some valuable prizes for the best grades in deportment made by students in the goverment school. For the one making the best grade during this term a choice of a graduating scholarship in Draughons Business Colleges or the McKinney College of McKinney, Texas; and suitable and valuable prizes for the other contestants. This prize is open for competition to every student of any grade, and virtually means that the tuition of the winner will be payed through the college from entrance to graduation—provided the student enters college sometime within the next five years

*ARTICLES ABOUT THE ESTABLISHMENT OF A
PUBLIC SCHOOL AT HOFFMAN*

*Top Left: April 5, 1906; Top Right: May 24, 1906;
Bottom Right: April 12, 1906*

Top: Hoffman School in 1919

*Bottom: Teacher with a group
of students in 1914*

Boys Basketball Team of 1917

*Girls Basketball Team playing on the old dirt court
at Hoffman School - Around 1920*

CHURCHES AND CLERGYMEN

For a town of its size and economic circumstances, Hoffman was always supported a good number of churches. In the mid-thirties, for example, there were at least five (and possibly six) churches, three (or four) attended by whites and two attended by blacks. Many clergymen of the day were either laymen who felt the call to preach or traveling preachers operating out of home churches in larger towns. Over the years, there were only a few full-time preachers. Only a smattering of them are mentioned by name in the pages that follow.

During Hoffman's early days, some of the local preachers used to give inspirational presentations in the schools as well as in their churches. This was often the case before the separation of church and state became an issue in public schools. In addition, Summer Vacation Bible School was a popular activity for many of Hoffman's children. A great deal of community life revolved around the churches, and even today many former residents still treasure their youthful memories of the time they spent involved in church activities.

The First Baptist Church of Hoffman was constructed in 1907 on land purchased from a Creek Indian landowner at a cost of $150.00 when Hoffman was still part of Indian Territory. The building was financed by the Home Mission Board of the Southern Baptist Convention of Atlanta, Georgia. It was constructed on lots 13 and 14 of block 26, and the church trustees who signed the loan agreement on June 28 of 1907 were I. C. Carloss, L. A. Chatham, and L. H. Davis. Under various part-time pastors, the First Baptist Church is still active in Hoffman today. It is located on the grounds of the old public school, in the building that served as the last Hoffman Grade School.

Several other churches were active in Hoffman over the years. Community Baptist Church was in town for many years, located in the building originally constructed and occupied by the First Baptist Church. From 1933 to 1942, there was an Assembly of God Church in Hoffman, and, at some point during the thirties and forties, there was also a Pentecostal Holiness Church. It was located on Main Street between the Stackhouse Drug Store and a shoe store. There were also at least two black churches in early Hoffman.

Many different preachers, pastors, and dedicated laymen and laywomen labored long and hard on behalf of their flocks in Hoffman over the years, far too many for all of them to be mentioned in this book. The career experience of one pastor, however, is profiled to provide a general picture of the kind of life that many of them led.

John Henry Porter, or "Preacher Porter," as he was called back then, pastored an Assembly of God Church in Hoffman from 1933 to 1942. He was born in Salyersville, Kentucky, on October 6, 1899. He arrived in Oklahoma at 18 years of age, first settling southeast of Muskogee in the Town of Brushy Mountain. While there he met a young lady by the name of Maudie Lee Alford, and they were married on October 4, 1920.

Sometime during the next few years, Porter gave his heart to God and was baptized. It was in 1929 that he first felt the call to preach. Shortly thereafter, he began to travel from town to town to hold revival meetings. After several successful years as a revivalist, he served as Pastor of Assembly of God Churches in Morris and Council Hill. He moved to Hoffman in 1933, and served as pastor there until 1942, when he moved to Henryetta. He died there on November 13, 1974. His wife Maude, or "Maudie", lived in Henryetta until she, too, died. The Porter's had 14 children, but only one of them, their son Elmer, was born in Hoffman. Elmer attended Hoffman School, and then served in the military during World War II. He was killed while on military duty.

Reverend Porter is perhaps remembered by former residents of Hoffman as much or more for his pastoral work as for the role he played in an unforgettable incident in which one of the town's leading merchants, C. E. Lackey, was killed during an argument that took place in his own general store on Main Street. (The incident is more fully described in another section of this book.) Although the effect of his passing was in no way quantifiable, the death of C. E. Lackey was widely thought of as an event that had an adverse economic impact on the health of Hoffman Townsite.

Of four churches that used to be active in Hoffman, two were attended mainly by whites (Hoffman Baptist Church and the Community Baptist Church) and two were attended mainly by blacks (the Pilgrim Baptist Church and the Church of God). All four congregations were energetically engaged in reaching out to members of the community.

Black church baptismal service in the early 1900s

*White church baptismal service at Carr Creek in 1903,
Preacher Fairchild of the Free Will Baptist Church presiding.*

*Kathleen Orendorff and a friend
at The Hoffman Baptist Church*

Reverend J. J. Kendricks and wife Wanda
in front of The Hoffman Baptist Church

Preacher John Henry Porter
and Wife Maudie in 1938

HOTELS, RESTAURANTS
AND LEASABLE BUSINESS SPACE

In September of 1904, a man by the name of H. Knight arrived in Hoffman from Arkansas. He built the first hotel in Hoffman, a two-story building that fronted Broadway and offered a room and an *"all you can eat home-cooked meal"* for $1 per night. The name of the hotel, if it had a business name other than Mr. Knight's surname, could not be found.

In 1905, an operation called The Hoffman Business Building was constructed in town. Owned and managed by G. E. Carney and H. Ritterhoff, it was the first building in Hoffman to offer leasable business space. One business occupant was the owners' own Hoffman House Hotel, with the office on the first floor serving as a lobby and rooms on the second floor of the building serving as guest rooms. The Hoffman House Hotel was billed as "an up-to-date concern that offered rooms for $2 per day." The building had two lower rooms measuring 50 by 50 feet that fronted Broadway Street, a center room that faced Main Street, and a 30 by 50 north room that also faced Main. The second floor of the building was cut into large, well ventilated, and nicely furnished rooms, some of which were used as sleeping quarters for patrons of the Hoffman House Hotel and some of which were used by other tenants of the establishment. Among the early tenants (in addition to the Hotel) were the John West & Son Hardware Store, Dr. O. T. Wright's drug store, and Dr. Harris.

In addition to the meal service offered by the two hotels in business in Hoffman at various times, a man by the last name of Porter once operated a place called Porter's Restaurant. The exact period of years his business was active is not known, but one of his employees was a woman by the name of Mildred Lewis. The restaurant was located on Main Street, between 1938 and 1942. Little else is known about the operation. There were never many restaurants in Hoffman, even during the best of times.

*The Hoffman House Business Building
owned by Carney and Ritterhoff*

Advertisement of rooms at The Hoffman House

*Ethel "Etta" England at the Odd Fellows Lodge
in Hoffman, Oklahoma. NOTE: This photograph was
not taken until 1948.*

The Knight Hotel

The Hunt Merchantile Company

FARMERS, RANCHERS, TENANT FARMERS AND SHARECROPPERS

Farming or ranching was the principal occupation of most of the early residents of the Hoffman area. The desire to own land was the primary force that drew most people to town in the first place, and a few residents were able to build successful agricultural operations over the years. Far more, however, struggled to eke an existence out of the small dry land farms and ranches operated in the area.

Cotton, of course, was a principal crop at Hoffman Townsite, as it was throughout the south. Corn was another major crop. Hoffmanites often grew and milled their own grain or had it ground by a local miller. A number of different grain milling operations existed in town over the years. Few records and only a single photograph of one of them, however, could be found.

Farm and ranch life in the years between 1905 and 1929 revolved around hard work and a considerable amount of isolation, and family gatherings were a major part of life in those days. One of the most common forms of social interaction was relatives visited one another as a pastime, and many extended families and neighbors, often closely interrelated, spent a lot of time together.

One successful rancher in the Hoffman area during the early 1900s was Ross Smith. Photographs of his home and some of his family appear on the pages that follow. It is interesting to note that one of the full-blood Creek Indian cowboys who worked on his place, a man by the name of Senora Burgess, became well known as a championship rodeo performer in Winnipeg, Canada, in 1913.

Unfortunately, however, most Hoffmanites did not become as successful in agriculture as they had hoped. Tenant farming and sharecropping became a fundamental fact of life in the early days of the town, as was the case in much of the South. Many whites were too poor to save enough capital to buy their own land, and most blacks were even worse off still. Having no land and little money and with only their labor to offer, many of Hoffman's poorest citizens, blacks as well as whites, were effectively forced into tenancy or sharecropping whether they liked it or not. Many of those who did own their own land had received it through government programs as allotments provided to create homesteads for the local Creek Indian and ex-slave population or by inheritance from those who did. Similarly, some whites and mixed bloods became landowners by inter-marriage with Indians or blacks who had received a government land allotment.

Under the sharecropping system, a farm family made a contract with a landlord. They became temporary land users, agreeing to pay for the use of the land with a share of the crop they produced. The landlord supplied the tools and seeds and provided the tenant farmers with the land, a mule, and a house or shack to live in. And, since these people usually had little or no money, they often had to buy their groceries, seed, implements, and other necessities on credit at stores that were often owned by the same landlords who owned their farms. Some local merchants even coined money that could only be exchanged in their own stores. The effect of such an arrangement was to lock families into a system whereby the crops they produced to sell each year were always mortgaged in advance, and that year after year that the value of their crop was less than the bill, plus interest, that they had run up at the local store. Some wound up effectively locked up in a form of indenture they often did not understand and from which they were effectively powerless to escape.

Tenant farmers operated on leased or rented land, but they were often not much better off than the sharecroppers. Many of them stayed deeply in debt to local landowners and merchants and barely made a living. Given the laws and customs of the times, tenant and sharecropper families were effectively prevented from leaving their rented homesteads if they owed money to anyone. Many were never able to dig their way out of debts that tended to increase with each passing year, and they became trapped in the system. For some the cycle was broken only when they were effectively forced off the land as farm prices collapsed during the Great Depression in later years.

Cutting hay on the Wilson farm
Hoffman, Oklahoma in 1903

Ross Smith (left), owner of the Smith Ranch
North of Hoffman, and his cousin Bud Smith -- 1910s

Cowboys working the Ross Smith Ranch
north of Hoffman in 1912

*Senora S. Burgess, a Creek Indian cowboy
who worked on the Ross Smith Ranch in 1911*

*Ethel "Ette" England at the Square Deal
Grist Mill during World War I*

LUMBERYARDS, SAWMILLS AND
COTTON GINS

Sawmills and lumber operations existed in Hoffman from the town's earliest days, but no photographs or business records of them could be found. The stands of commercially harvestable timber in the area were not large, and just as soon as possible the mills probably cut out as the best of what was there to be taken. At least for a while, fine walnut lumber valued at as much as $300 was taken out of the nearby Deep Fork River bottom each day. For the times, that was a lot of money.

J. W. Brown, formerly of Sioux City, Iowa, who arrived in Hoffman in June of 1904, opened the Brown Lumber Company in August of that same year. By 1905, he was carrying goods in stock valued at over $5,000 to satisfy the demands of his patrons.

Jackson Brothers Lumber, a similar business, was in operation in by 1906. It was owned by a Mr. Jackson, who moved to Hoffman from Henryetta shortly after the town was opened. His family stayed in Henryetta so that his children could continue in school there, but in 1906 he planned to make Hoffman his eventual home. Whether he did or not is unknown.

As early as 1906, a man by the name of Henry Rice operated a sawmill in Hoffman. No records of his business could be found.

W. A. Anthony ran a sawmill operation in town as late as the 1930s. In addition to his sawmill, Anthony also owned and either operated or rented out several other businesses, leased commercial properties, and rented farmland in the area.

Cotton was a principal crop at Hoffman Townsite. At least two cotton gins were operated there at one time during its early days, the Choctaw Gin Company and the Berge and Forbes Company. Their earliest owners were not determinable, but a man by the name of Scott Lockhart may have owned one of them. Over the years, both gins went through several changes of ownership. John Tate once operated a gin in Hoffman, and, during parts of the 1930s and 1940s, Jack Pyle owned and operated the only cotton gin still in operation at the time. The gin Pyle operated was located at the corner of Broadway and Davis Streets, on the southwest corner of the intersection on the site where a lumberyard once stood. The Pyle family lost both their cotton gin and their personal home to a tornado in 1960.

Every day almost there are hundreds of dollars' worth of fine walnut timber being shipped out of this country, that shauld be manufactured right here where they grow. True, the marketing of these logs furnish a very good business for those who handle them, but our people derive only a small portion of the profit. If this timber was sawed, planed and made into furniture right here, it would furnish work for all the unimployed and at the same time it would keep the money at home where it belongs. If it will pay to ship this material to a mill hundreds of miles away, why will it not pay to manufacture it here where it is produced and thus save the freight expense?

ARTICLE ENCOURAGING ADVANCEMENT
OF THE TIMBER INDUSTRY
APRIL 12, 1906

FOR A TIME AT HOFFMAN,
CISTERNS WERE FAR MORE COMMON
THAN WATER WELLS

GENERAL MERCHANDISERS, DRY GOODS STORES AND GROCERS

Many different grocery and dry goods stores existed in Hoffman over the years, and some of them went through many changes of ownership. The second permanent business building in town, for example, was William Hoover's grocery store. Another grocery, Carpenter & Varner's, was once located on Broadway. In addition, the Hays and Welch Market once offered fresh meat and groceries to residents.

W. W. Buchanan once operated a business called the Pioneer Hardware Store in Hoffman. Buchanan arrived in Indian Territory in 1903, first settling in Henryetta and then moving to Hoffman when the town was opened for settlement. He located there in October of 1904, where he sold hardware and other home and farm implements.

An establishment called The Mumford Jewelry Store once operated in Hoffman. The specialties of the house were a line of jewelry and the repairing of watches and clocks. Little else is known about this business.

The only furniture store to operate in Hoffman was called John West & Son, a business that arrived on the scene in mid-1905. Actually, the owner bought out an even earlier businessman (name unknown) who operated only a short time as the Hoffman Furniture Company. Starting in March of 1905, the new owner later added hardware and implements to his line of merchandise. The business consisted of two large rooms fronting Broadway in the Hoffman House business building, the only purveyor of leasable business space in town at the time.

The Hunt Mercantile Company operated one store in Hoffman and another in Tulsa. Owned by Mr. Hunt and managed by J. L. Renner, it was promoted as "a large buyer and, therefore, a low seller." Their product line consisted of groceries, clothing, boot and shoes, and dry goods.

A man by the name of Ward once operated a grocery store in Hoffman, and a man by the name of C. B. Herman came to town from Missouri in November of 1906 to open the C. B. Herman Grocery and Hardware Store. Herman eventually disposed of his hardware line, putting in its place a line of boots, shoes, and dry goods.

A man by the name of Liesterfeltz moved to Hoffman from Muskogee to open the Ideal Hat Shop. His store offered a line of fine millinery goods. The business was in operation in the old post office building in 1906.

A member of the Ritterhoff family owned a dry goods and general merchandise store in Hoffman in 1915. Little information was available about this business.

At one time in the early 1920s, Sil Peters owned and operated a meat market in Hoffman and John and Minerva Spurlock operated Spurlock's Grocery and Dry Goods Store. The Farrell family operated Farrell's Grocery Store in Hoffman from 1938 to 1942.

The C. E. Lackey Building was a grocery and dry goods store located on the northeast corner of the intersection of Main and Broadway Streets during the 1930s and 1940s. Lackey also operated a slaughterhouse to supply his store with fresh meat. His slaughterhouse operation was located about one block from the store, staffed by butchers Alvin Crawford and Judd Allen. Buck Crawford preceded them as the butcher.

During the 1930s, C. E. Lackey and W. A. Anthony were competitors in the grocery and dry goods business. Lackey owned much of the business space on the east side of Main Street while Anthony owned much of the same kind of property on the west side of the street. Both men operated grocery stores as well as other kinds of businesses, in addition to renting business, residential, and farm properties. They were among the town's wealthiest citizens in those times. Charley E. Lackey built the C. E. Lackey Store, which was the last one of the old commercial buildings that once stood in Hoffman. When it burned down, the Hoffman Community Center was built on its old slab. The Center is still in service today, under the management of long-term resident Ruby Burney.

Jack Pyle bought out C. E. Lackey's grocery in the 1930s and operated it until the 1940s when he was bought out himself by one of his former employees, Paul Hutchison. Hutchison had owned a different grocery store in Hoffman before he bought Lackey's operation.

TOP LEFT: RITTERHOFF''S GENERAL STORE, AROUND 1915
Pictured: Opal Thomas. Ritterhoff's was located across the
street from Spurlock's (later Peter's) General Store

TOP RIGHT: THE IDEAL HAT SHOP IN 1918
Pictured: Ida Wilson (left) and a
friend (name unknown)

Herman's Store Advertisement

*Members of the Buchannan Family,
owners of Buchannan's Hardware*

BUCHANAN'S HARDWARE STORE
The store, which was opened in 1904, was located on the northwest corner of Fourth and Broadway; the advertisement at the bottom was placed in the Hoffman Herald in 1906. Courtesy of the Henryetta Historical Society of Henryetta, Oklahoma.

*LEE STEVENSON (TOP RIGHT), OWNER OF
STEVENSON'S GROCERY STORE*

*Stevenson's Grocery Story was on the west side of Main Street, with the
owner's living quarters upstairs.   Pictured are Lee and Mamie
(Freeman) Stevenson (top row), shown here with Lloyd Calhoun
Freeman, Mamie's Father, and his Daughter Blanche (Freeman)
Baker at a family function around 1903.*

MUMFORD WATCH MAKER AND JEWELER'S AD

Hoffman — 1911 to 1918

6th St.

5th St.

BRIDGE

RAVINE

?

Pa Chatham, postmaster

Forest Chatham rural mailman

Ritterhoff

Buchanan's Hardware and Embalming, later a Picture Show

?

MAIN

Feed Store

Living quarters upstairs

Stevenson's Grocery Store

Post Office

Dr. Carloss Office-Druggist

Schultz Mercantile

Myers' Bank

RAVINE

STREET

BRIDGE

Water Well

BROADWAY

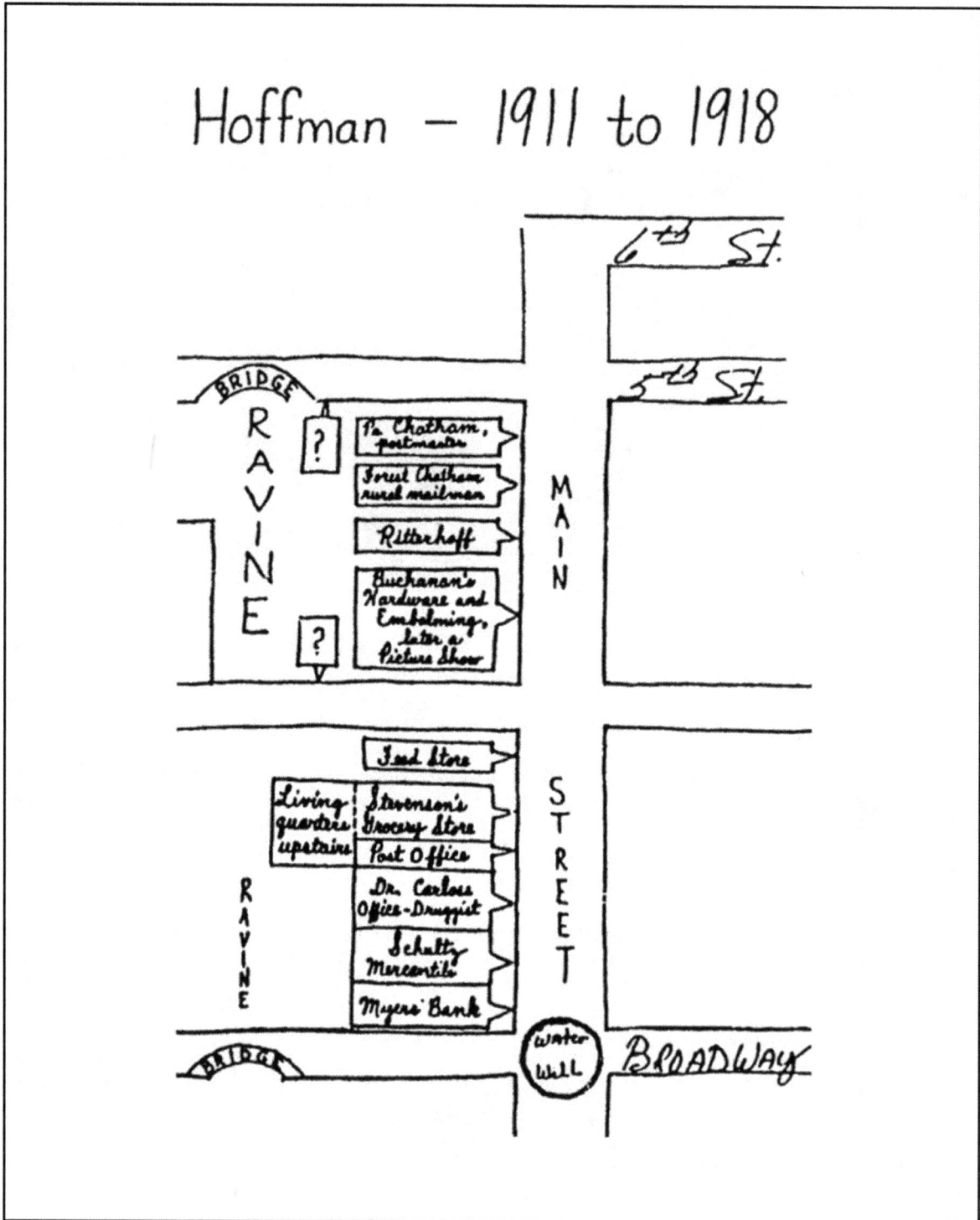

Hand-drawn map of Hoffman from 1911 to 1918, showing the location of Stevenson's Grocery Store and Buchannan's Hardware on the east side of Main Street

Spurlock's Store -- Around 1920
Pictured: Owners John and Minerva Spurlock

Brown's Lumber Advertisement

MERCHANT ADVERTISEMENTS

At Actual Cost

Men's Underwear

Wool Blankets.

500lb Best Patent Flour at per hundred, $1.90

Still Stocked With

Barton Bro's Shoes.

Shults & Turner.

John West & Son,

Dealers in

Shell and Heavy

HARDWARE.

Leaders For Low Pricer.

Hoffman, I. T.

MERCHANT ADVERTISEMENTS

For First-Class and superior Finish WE HAVE ON HAND

Marbleized Wood, Oak Mantle Office, and Mission Clocks, Consisting of the LEADING MAKES.   Cheap as the Cheapest.

Expert Watch, Clock and Jewelry Repairing.

When Others Fail, Try Us.

Satisfaction guaranteed or No Pay.

F. J. MUMFORD,

Watch-Maker and Jeweler.

S. MAIN ST.   HOFFMAN, I. T.

Joe Habiger will leave at once for St. Louis where he will look for a business location. If he does not find anything to suit him there he will go to Washington or Oregon. Mr. Habiger invested considerable money in the new town of Hoffman, Okla., but decided he did not like it there on account of the "niggers" and chills.—Hoisington (Kansas) Dispatch.

The above little fling is a fair sample of what a diseased brain can manufacture. The editor of this paper knows Mr. Habiger, and knowing him as we do, we know that he never even intimated that his reasons for not comming here were as above stated. We have been a resident of Hoffman since last February, and haven't had a chill, nor have we even saw a person that has had one, and as to the "niggers," we want to inform the Dispatch editor that there are fewer here than there are in his county seat town and that they are a better class of people to boot. As a rule they own their own homes and mind their own business and are even more gentlemanly than to make such an assertion about anybody, as that gotton off by the Dispatch. Mr. Habiger owns property in Hoffman and his reason for not going into business here was purely on account of church accomodations, and not on account of any dislike for the town or its people.

If the Dispatch man will come down we will show him that our "niggers" are respectable black men and women; that our Indians do not cover their nakedness with blankets or carry any pale face scalps around with them, but instead, are educated, refined and eminently fitted to appear in the best of society; that our whites are not outlaws and that our location is not an incubator of fever, chills or ague.

All the people of the Territory ask is a square deal—if you must write us up, first come and see and then paint things as they really are, and not as your prejudiced imagination suggests them. WE HAVE THE GOODS, and will take pleasure in showing them.

We realize that to tell the truth, the whole truth and nothing but the truth about this country would work a great hardship on the big landlords of the north and eastern states, who from year to year are growing more wealthy off the labor of their renters, who give the greater part of the income from their toil for the privilege of living, while if they knew the truth about the opportunities of the New South they would come here and own as good or a better home of their own.

If the Dispatch editor is an honorable man and not a stranger to the truth, he will correct the bad impression created by his little fling, by publishing the facts as set forth in this article; if he is not, then he will reply by another dirty squib which will lower him in the estimation of those who know both him and the humble Irishman who penns these lines.

This article, critical of former Hoffmanite Joe Habiger, more clearly describes attitudes of his times than its writer understood!

BARBERSHOPS, HONKYTONKS
AND POOLHALLS

At one time, there were two barbershops in Hoffman. George Martin operated a two-chair shop in 1927, offering haircuts and shaves and the added attraction of a pool table. He rented his shop space from a man by the name of Sil Peters, and he employed one barber in addition to himself. The shop was located across the street from C. E. Lackey's store and about 100 yards north, near where the post office was located at the time. Martin's barber shop and pool table for a time became a frequent watering hole for some of the local men, and some old timers can attest to at least one murder and several fistfights that took place there.

George Jackson Martin, who, like many sons of the South, may have been named after General "Stonewall" Jackson, moved to Hoffman in the early 1900s from his home State of Arkansas, where his father had been a preacher. It was said that he arrived in town under circumstances so suspicious that his neighbors shied away from confrontation with him, and it was rumored that he had left Arkansas in the middle of the night and that he had personally known Belle Starr. No one knew exactly what deep secret was hidden in his past, but he came across as a quiet and dignified man that most people liked and trusted and did not want to alienate. One of his idiosyncrasies was that he almost never washed his hair, believing that not washing it would keep it from thinning as he grew older.

Called "The Colonel" by those who knew him well, he earned a living by trading in livestock and implements, gardening, doing piece work jobs, and hunting and fishing in the local area--and, at least for a time, running a barbershop. He could barely read and write, and throughout his life he never held a regular salaried job. In the twenties, George married Virginia Victoria McFarlin, whose father, George Washington McFarlin, came to Hoffman from Fort Smith, Arkansas. Virginia could not read or write. George and Virginia eventually had six children, all of whom attended school in Hoffman. Their names were William (or "Dub"), Charley, Robert, Dempsey, Naomi, and George, Jr.

Between 1938 and 1942, a Mr. Faye also operated a barbershop located on Main Street in Hoffman. His shop space was rented from C. E. Lackey, but no additional information about his shop could be found. The popular consensus is that his was the last barbershop in Hoffman.

Although little solid information about it could be found, a man by the name of Peter Cole once operated a Billiard and Pool Parlor in Hoffman. Another man, Neal Easley, operated a place that people called "Neal's Honkytonk" during the 1930s and 1940s. Neal's was located near a dirt ball field (not the one on the school grounds) that was used for community recreation, mainly by older white and colored men. During its day, it was the site of a number of drunken revelries, bar fights, stabbings, and even murders.

Making liquor and beer was a common activity throughout the region during most of Hoffman's existence, and bootlegging was widely practiced throughout the Thirties and Forties. Homemade beer and bootleg whiskey (or "White Lightning," as it was called) was sold from under the counter out of a good number of otherwise respectable retail dry goods and grocery establishments as well as the more unsavory honkytonks.

Gambling was very popular among some of the men of Hoffman, especially dice and card games. In addition to the local bars and some hotels, the town jail was one place on a Friday or Saturday night where a game often could be found. Prisoners would play on the ground through the bars with any locals who showed up to keep them company.

Another vice of the times that has somewhat declined in terms of widespread popularity today was the use of tobacco in the form of snuff and chewing tobacco. Cigarettes and cigars have long been popular tobacco products, but the home and business spittoons that were prevalent during the early days of Hoffman have long since gone by the wayside. In those days, many women as well as men dipped snuff and went about spitting out tobacco juice a bit more often than we would find tolerable today.

Yet another notorious illicit activity of the time was prostitution, which took place in the back or upper rooms of bars, hotels and boarding houses and often featured women brought in for short term stints from larger cities such as Tulsa. No one claimed to know much about it at the time, but it happened, albeit sporadically, just the same.

BLACKSMITHS, LIVERYMEN, DRAYMEN AND MECHANICS

A man by the name of Fred Williams operated one of the earliest blacksmith shops in Hoffman, starting there in the 1910s. He was followed by Tom Johnson in later years, and landowner and merchant Charlie Lackey owned and leased a blacksmith shop there in the 1930s. A man named John Lewis ran the shop for him. In addition, Tom Johnson also kept another blacksmith shop open in Hoffman from 1920 to 1939.

A white settler by the name of Jason Perry "Frank" Wilson, who was born in Michigan, moved to Hoffman in the early 1900s to open and operate Frank Wilson's Livery Stable on South Main Street past Broadway. He ran a freight hauling business and rented horse-drawn buggies, wagons, saddle horses, and horse-drawn wagons for business and pleasure and for hauling heavy loads. Wilson and his wife were long-term residents of Hoffman who became very successful in business.

Hoffman's drayman in 1906 was a man by the name of J. Kinyon, about whom little information was available. His business was to move heavy private and commercial cargos using horse- and mule-drawn wagon teams.

As blacksmithing declined and automobiles gained in popularity, mechanics started to become active in Hoffman. Charlie Edwards and his son Bill, for example, established a garage in town during the 1930s, and other such businesses were in operation there even earlier.

A commercial hauling job of the early 1900s
by Frank Wilson's Livery-Drayage business

*Advertisements by two of Wilson Livery's Competitors,
The Hoffman Dray and Transfer Line and Nelson and Gash's
Hoffman Livery and Feed Barn*

Simpson's Blacksmithing Service

*Mechanic Charlie Edwards and
his Son Bill at Edward's Garage*

TOP: COMMUNITY WELL AT THE INTERSECTION OF MAIN AND
BROADWAY IN 1979. BOTTOM: THE OLD TOWN JAIL.
NOTE: By the time these pictures were taken, both the well and the jail,
after having been repaired many times, had fallen to ruin.

PHYSICIANS AND DRUGGISTS

One of the earliest physicians in Hoffman was Dr. O. T. Wright, whose office was located in the north room of the Hoffman House Business Building. His office faced Main Street and was also featured a drug store. Dr. Wright arrived in Hoffman from Missouri to start his drug business, first locating in a small house on Main Street and then moving to the Hoffman House.

Around the same time, a suite of rooms on the second floor of the Hoffman House business building was occupied as office space by another physician, Dr. A. W. Harris. Not much about his operation could be found.

During the 1930s, Dr. Hudson operated a drug store and held forth as a general practitioner out of an office that was located on Main Street. His residence was located at the intersection of 5th and Oak Streets. Until a few years after World War II when he retired, Dr. Hudson practiced medicine in Okmulgee, Oklahoma.

Dr. Carloss operated a drug store and kept an office on West Broadway Street. During the 1930s, he moved his office to the town of Morris, where he continued to practice until after World War II. When he lived in Hoffman, his residence was also located on West Broadway.

The Stackhouse Drug Store, owned by W. L. Stackhouse, was in business in Hoffman during the 1940s. The building his store was in later burned down, and when it was restored it housed the new Hoffman Post Office.

Chatham Drug Company

*Physician's billing for services rendered by home visitation
on horseback in 1914. W. S. Hudson, M.D., was local surgeon
for the Missouri, Oklahoma & Gulf Railroad.*

CHAPTER IV

HOFFMAN
THROUGH THE YEARS

From small and humble beginnings, Hoffman grew with a rush that, according to civic booster O. E. O'Bleness, editor of the Hoffman Herald, "had few equals in the annals of town building." Within a six-month period, for example, over forty different businesses (and over one-hundred residences) were built and occupied in Hoffman, indeed a very respectable spurt of growth given the general remoteness of the area and other conditions and standards of those times.

The first permanent home ever constructed at the townsite, again according to O. E. O'Bleness, was built by H. A. and C. C. Chatham. The Chatham's came to town from La Monte, Missouri, in 1905 to open the Chatham Drug Store that was once located on Broadway Street. Their home was located (as far as anyone could recall) at the southwest corner of Main and 5th Streets. This family was very typical of the many that came to Hoffman in search of business opportunity and property ownership during the promising early days of townsite development.

Life in what the early settlers called the "Promised Land" seemed to be as good as could be expected all the way through the 1910s and 1920s. Even before the time Oklahoma became the forty-sixth State of the United States on November 16, 1907, Hoffman Townsite, for example, was already a thriving little railroad town in what was once called the "Cotton Belt." Located just east of the town of Henryetta and about 70 miles south of Tulsa near a depot on the KO&G Railroad line, it had a downtown area lined with businesses and offices--including a post office, a newspaper, two banks, several general merchandise retail stores, a millinery shop, a blacksmith, several grocery stores, a meat market, two doctor's offices, a drug store, an embalmer, a hotel and restaurant, a rooming house, a livery stable, churches, and a school.

The future held exciting possibilities, and Hoffman's settlers had high hopes of cashing in on the promises held out by the investors, developers and promoters of the general area and of the Townsite. In some photographs of the early days there, the feeling of optimism and confidence that prevailed back then is easily seen in the faces of the people. It was not until the beginning of the 1930s that things began to change for the worse.

Thousands of people have lived in Hoffman over the years, and the legal ownership of both residential and business properties has changed many times. Some families stayed in the town or surrounding area for just a short time, but others have lived in the area since the townsite was first developed. A small sampling of life at the townsite appears in the pages that follow.

JOHN ENGLAND, SENIOR
John England was a pre-statehood game trapper and,
later on in life, oil field worker. His wife, Ethel,
was a midwife at Hoffman.

Hunters Charlie Carpenter (Right) and Friend
(name unknown) -- Around 1915

*Manual "John" Furr taught at Hoffman School
from 1930 to 1932*

*Lillie and daughter Tina "Tiny" Mae Quinton at Quinton's
Grocery, Gas Station, and Garage at Wildcat Junction in 1938*

*Wilma Jean (left) and Helena Hood at Farrell's Grocery Store
on Main Street in 1938*

*Jess Quinton and son James
at the Hoffman Cotton Gin in 1932*

*Rural Mail Carrier P. L. Orendorff
at Hoffman in the 1930s*

TOP LEFT: Merchant Charlie E. Lackey, Owner of the C. E. Lackey Store. TOP RIGHT: Charles "Little Charles" Lackey, son of Hoffman Merchant Charlie E. Lackey. BOTTOM LEFT: Charlie and Stella Lackey. BOTTOM RIGHT: Charlie E. Lackey with daughters Brunell (left) and Inez in 1931.

The northwest corner of the intersection of Main and Broadway Streets of Hoffman, Oklahoma, in 1937. Lackey's store in the background. Pictured: Jimmy Wilson and friend (name unknown). Notice that the business is referred to as a "trading company".

Advertisement by Lackey's Store

TOP LEFT: Merchant W. A. "Zant" Anthony, owner of Anthony's Store. TOP RIGHT: W. A. "Zant" Anthony and wife Viola, around 1934. BOTTOM LEFT: Arley and Marie (Horne) Anthony. Arley was one of W. A. Anthony's sons. BOTTOM RIGHT: Jerry Lee Anthony and mother Frances Garret.

W. A. ANTHONY'S STORE
For a time, the Hoffman Post Office was
housed in a corner of this building.

HOFFMAN SCHOOL TEACHERS IN 1936-37
Bryan Boatmun, Laura Lennox, Roxie Evans, Lenna
Nicholson and Delmar R. Didlake.

The Hoffman Hornets Under 100 Pound
Boys Basketball Team of 1938-39

Hoffman School Carnival Queen
Joyce Bowden in 1934

Hoffman High School Class of 1938

*School bus driver Sam Cunningham
1937-38 School Year*

Wash day in the Orendorff's back yard

Percy and Etta Orendorff and their children
Darden (top right), Kathleen and Milton

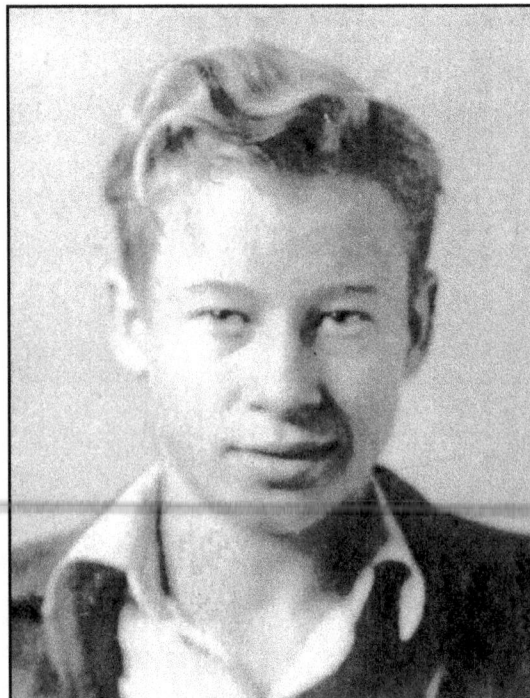

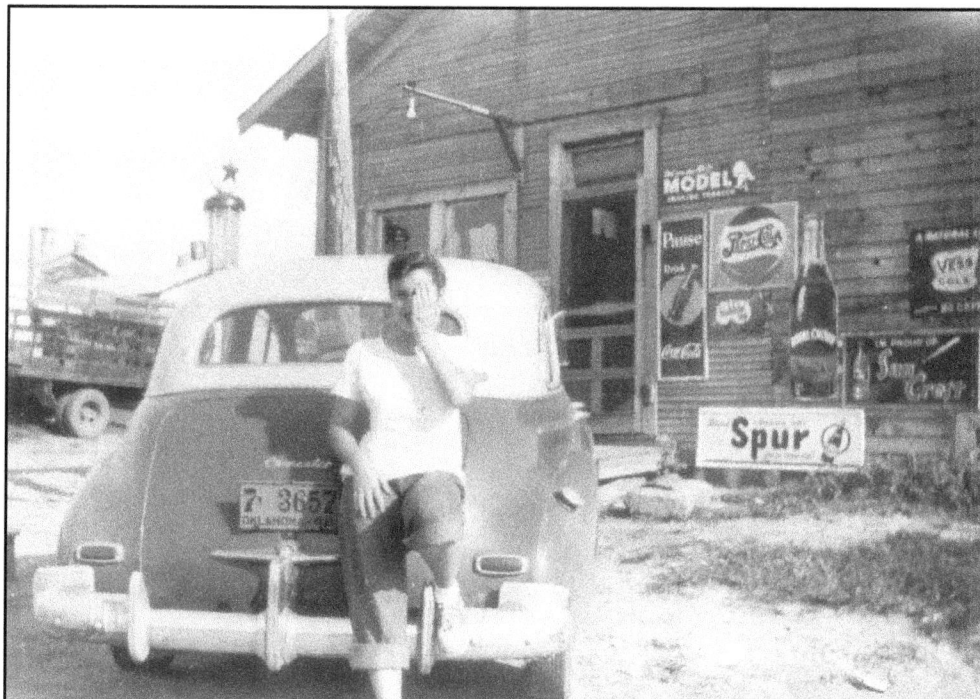

HUTCHISON'S STORE
The was the first of two stores Paul Hutchison operated in Hoffman.

LEFT: *Cecil Lewis, sitting with two colored separate school students.*
RIGHT: *Emma Lou Parker, age 18, and Johnny Quinton in 1942.*

HOFFMAN SCHOOL TEACHERS IN 1938

HOFFMAN HIGH SCHOOL CLASS OF 1939

TOP LEFT: Elmer Porter in 1943, one of many young men of Hoffman who served in the nation's armed forces during World War II. Assigned to the U.S.S. Suwannee, he was killed in action in the South Pacific on November 1, 1944. TOP RIGHT: Gladys Moffett; BOTTOM: Cecil and one-time postmaster Leveta Lewis.

*Squirrel hunters George Jackson Martin
and Son Robert, around 1945*

*Tressie (Tinney) Phillips, Bill Phillips, and Robert Martin
butchering a hog on the Martin farm in 1949*

HOFFMAN GRAMMAR SCHOOL -- AROUND 1934
Voncile Ferguson (blond on the horse), Velma Ferguson (on the horse), and Lelan Ferguson at the Hoffman Grammar School. The rock building at the right housed the cistern.

HOFFMAN GRAMMAR SCHOOL --1947-48
This building was constructed during the 1947-48 school year by local businessman W. A. "Zant" Anthony. It was built on the foundation of the WPA-built grade school that was destroyed by fire during the 1945-46 school year.

*Aerial view of the Hoffman Elementary School (left) and
Hoffman High School and Gymnasium in May of 1960*

CHAPTER V

THE YEARS OF TOWNSITE DECLINE

INTRODUCTION

From the 1930s onward, Hoffman began to decline as an economically viable townsite. While there was no single reason for its decline, some identifiable events or conditions clearly contributed to its problems. Some of these events were obvious, but others were much more subtle. Among the most obvious was the rash of economic problems that beset the national economy beginning in the 1930s.

Even in the best of times life for the average resident of the town would probably never have been described as easy, but the plain and modest wood frame buildings in the community must have seemed especially stark and bare during the trying period in our national history known as the Great Depression. It was the single most devastating economic blow to affect the town.

Popularly thought of as being caused by the stock market crash of 1929, the Great Depression is better attributed to a combination of contributing factors rather than any one force or activity. But regardless of its cause, Hoffman--like most other parts of the country--was deeply affected by both the problems and the solutions that ensued. Furthermore, due to its immersion in the agricultural problems caused by what came to be known as the Dust Bowl, Hoffman's cup nearly ran over with economic hardship during the 1930s and 1940s.

THE GREAT DEPRESSION
OF THE 1930s

Hoffmanites were as unprepared as the rest of the country for the depression that traumatized our country in the 1930s. After having recovered from the recession that followed the first World War, the national economy had begun to boom in the 1920s. By the late 1920s people across the country were caught up in what was called "prosperity fever." With the exception of unskilled workers and small farmers (of which there were a good number in Hoffman), most Americans thought that the future looked better than it had in years.

The stock market crash of 1929 is generally considered to be the event that initiated the series of problems that led to the Great Depression of the 1930s. The "Great Crash" caught the country by surprise, but the forces that caused it had been building for many years.

Wages had been increasing at the same time that business profits had been moving steadily upward. Given such prosperous conditions, people felt safe about spending more and more money. There was a binge of buying of consumer goods such as cars, appliances, and furniture. With the great demand for goods, business boomed for the nation's factories and stores.

With money on hand and credit readily available, people also began to buy shares of stock in fast-growing companies in order to cash in on what seemed to be a foolproof stock market. With conditions as they were, people felt confident enough to borrow money to buy stocks "on the margin," or on credit. It seemed safe--and even wise--to buy stocks on credit when there seemed to be good evidence of continued business prosperity. Even reputable brokers and bankers became, in effect, speculators in a totally unregulated stock market, and all the demand combined to push the price of shares ever higher at the stock exchanges.

Many people who had never invested before (much less speculated) in the stock markets got caught up in the "get rich quick" attitude of the times. Many invested all they had saved in stock market investments. Eventually, however, stock prices peaked at what was a clearly unrealistic high, and then began a dramatic fall downward. An atmosphere of instability and uncertainty seemed to take over the financial community, and eventually the events of what came to be called "Black Thursday" and "Terrible Tuesday" hit the markets.

Suddenly, everyone wanted to sell stock shares rather than buy new ones. Prices began to drop like a rock as panic selling flooded the market. Stocks were exchanged at triple the normal rate, but some shares could not be sold at any price because buyers were uncertain of their reasonable value. Everyone wanted to sell, but no one wanted to buy. Ultimately, the result was that thousands of shareholders, stockbrokers, banker, and business owners lost everything they had invested in the market.

The great stock market crash is now considered to have been the major event that began the worst economic crisis in our country's history--the Great Depression. As people in one segment of the economy became worried about their financial security, their decisions had a ripple effect on people in other segments of the economy. Those who had lost their savings in the stock market, for example, immediately had to cut back on all of their buying of consumer goods and services. Factory and retail stores then began to lose sales and, therefore, had to reduce the number of people they employed. With each type of cutback, the overall economic condition of the country became even worse. Things got so bad that companies began to go out of business, putting thousands more in the unemployment line. Without an income, even more people then had to reduce their spending.

In 1930, people all across the country had to make decisions to cut back on their level of economic activity in the form of personal buying and spending. Business profits soon turned to losses, factories shut down, and even more people lost their jobs. To make matters even worse, savings levels were so low that soon what was available to tide people over was used up. With no effective social safety net programs to help people ride out the storm, millions soon began to see that they faced a desperate situation. The so-called "domino effect" of the chain of events that occurred made many people feel that their situation was hopeless. With the same combination of events simultaneously affecting people all across the country, fear and even panic spread throughout the national economic system.

Even as all of this was going on, the country was hit by catastrophic agricultural problems. Due to high farm prices after World War I, many farmers had gone heavily into debt to buy more land and equipment to cash in on what had seemed to be lasting positive farm price conditions. When prices for farm goods went down due to over-production, many farmers made too little profit to be able to make their loan payments. More farm goods were being produced than the population could buy, forcing farm prices down and, therefore, pushed many farmers into bankruptcy.

Another situation that made our overall economic situation even worse was that a tariff passed by Congress in 1922 (the Fordney-McCumber Tariff) was so high that it effectively prevented foreign countries from repaying war debts because they could not sell their products to the American market to make income. This caused these foreign countries to retaliate against our country by raising their own tariffs. The restriction of trade that resulted worsened our overall economic situation even further, especially in the farming sector.

Yet another problem was that the Federal Reserve Bank did not increase the nation's money supply when doing so might have helped deal with our economic problems. Some banks, especially those in rural areas and in small towns, were weak and not well managed. When these banks got into serious trouble due to bad loans and having insufficient reserves to deal with their problems, they had no choice but to close down because there was no mechanism in place to help them ride out the bad times. When one bank failed, people became scared of banks in general and began to draw out their money at other banks. The additional bank failures that resulted were yet another blow to the economy.

A more subtle but nonetheless difficult economic problem in those days was that even though the productive capacity of American factories had grown rapidly after World War I, wages had risen more slowly than production and the price of goods. American companies had been producing more goods than could be consumed, especially considering the restrictions hampering overseas trade. The situation did not seem serious because it had been concealed by excessive consumer installment buying. There had actually been a decline in consumer purchasing power, and the overproduction led to even more factory layoffs.

The combined effect of all these separate problems caught our country unprepared. Throughout late 1929 and early 1930, the depression spread unchecked across the nation. By the end of 1930, over 4 million people were unemployed and there were no prospects of finding new employment in sight. Breadlines became common in cities across the country, and gloominess and desperation began to spread as the last savings of hundreds of thousands of people was quickly used up.

Everywhere problems and hardship seemed to grow. Our president at that time, Herbert Hoover, quickly became one of the most reviled and ridiculed men in America. He did not cause the depression, but he was clearly blamed for it. Homeless people who slept under newspapers were said to be wearing "Hoover blankets," the jack rabbits eaten by hungry people were called "Hoover hogs," and the shack villages that were built around most cities by homeless people were called "Hoovervilles."

Oklahoma in general was especially hard hit by the depression, and within the State the northeastern counties suffered as much and probably more than others. Several factors accounted for the negative difference. By 1930 some 62 percent of all farms in Oklahoma were tenant operated, but in the northeast eight counties exceeded that total by as much as 18 percent. At the same time, average farm income in the area was only $1018 per year, some 35 percent less than the State as a whole. Sadly, the average was only 42 percent of what it had been a decade earlier. Three successive droughts early in the 1930s only added to the misery already produced by inefficient tenant farming and the planting of half fertile soil.

Other sectors of Oklahoma's economy fared just as poorly. Between 1929 and 1934 petroleum production, most of which was in the northeastern counties, decreased by 30 percent. Lead and zinc mines closed and left thousands unemployed. Wages paid by manufacturers decreased by 20 percent between

1931 and 1933, significant in the northeast because of the economic importance of Tulsa. And from 1927 on, bank failures occurred with increasing rapidity in the northeastern counties.

Franklin D. Roosevelt was elected President of the United States on his promise to help America deal with the problems of the Great Depression. He surprised most of the nation, however, when he soon lived up to his word. Called the "New Dealers," the President and his advisers immediately went about devising a series of programs designed to provide quick relief to those devastated by the depression, to start the nation's industries on the road to recovery, and to take long-range steps to prevent another great depression from ever occurring.

When Roosevelt took office in 1933, about 13 million people, or about 25 percent of the labor force, were out of work, and many of these people had used up all of their personal savings and had sold all they owned to avoid outright starvation. Roosevelt opposed what was then called the "dole," or the giving of cash money to people, but he and his cabinet believed that drastic action had to be taken to head off the possibility of starvation that faced many of our people. In a relatively short period of time, he and his cabinet worked with Congress to pass the social legislation that was packaged and publicized as "The New Deal." The direct and indirect effects of this legislation on Hoffman Townsite were immediate and highly significant.

It is unlikely that the average Hoffmanite realized, much less truly appreciated, the extent of the effort at the time, but most of them were direct or indirect beneficiaries of the New Deal programs of the Roosevelt presidency. During a time when the unspoken law of the land was accurately encapsulated by the saying "Root, Hog, or die!" the President's famous series of "fireside chats"-- undertaken to remind Americans that they "had nothing to fear but fear itself"-- struck a responsive chord throughout Northeastern Oklahoma and, indeed, across the entire country.

Under one "alphabet agency" heading or another, many projects were implemented in Hoffman proper or in the surrounding area to deal effectively with the depression. These programs took on three basic forms--relief, recovery, and reform. The most immediate need was relief for the victims of the depression and for business recovery, but the President's longer ranged plans also included reform measures to ensure that another disastrous depression would not take place. It would be difficult to overstate the full impact of the Roosevelt administration's New Deal programs on Hoffman Townsite.

Congress established the Works Progress Administration, or WPA, on May 6, 1935, to employ people in useful local public works projects as a means of providing immediate employment to those on relief who could not find work elsewhere. Over time, more than 2 million were employed by the WPA in any given month in a variety of public works projects around the country. During its existence, the WPA spent more than $11 billion on 250,000 public projects around the nation. Though there was some wasted money and effort, the WPA provided a new start for many who would otherwise have remained unemployed.

Of the almost $12 billion the agency received, more that $185 million was expended in Oklahoma. In the State as elsewhere the WPA sponsored a number of different programs for the unemployed. Among these were the Federal Art Project, the Federal Writer's Project, the Historical Records Survey, the Federal Music Project, and the Federal Theater Project. Additionally, the WPA had programs for adult hospital aides. Few of these programs, however, were designed to provide employment for unskilled laborers, that class of persons who made up the largest percentage of the relief rolls in Oklahoma and its northeastern counties. For these individuals the WPA organized a massive construction program of public buildings and facilities. Because of its size of operation, the type of work it performed, and its 75 percent share of the total budget, the latter benefited more of Oklahoma's unemployed, had a greater impact socially, and left a physical legacy more apparent than the other programs.

The WPA in Oklahoma was entirely a federal government operation. Organized into one statewide, eight district and fourteen area offices, it was administered by officials who answered directly to supervisors in Washington, D.C. The agency determined eligibility of people seeking employment, selected workers of the type needed, set the wage scale to be paid, and saw to it that Federal Treasury checks were issued for work accomplished. Construction projects undertaken by the WPA were planned and sponsored by local governmental units, which also shared in the costs--an average of 25 percent statewide by 1940. Although there were exceptions, in general sponsors of these activities usually provided materials while the agency supplied a supervised labor force. National guidelines dictated that particular projects be "useful" and limited in cost to $52,000 exclusive of local matching funds or equivalencies.

Between 1935 and 1943, when the agency was abolished, the WPA public works program in Northeastern Oklahoma had undertaken a large number of state and locally sponsored projects. Most numerous were those involving construction of roads and streets, bridges, and culverts, and sidewalks and curbs. Equally impressive were those relating to sanitation and public health, especially malarial control ditches, sanitary privies, and water treatment and delivery systems. Other projects included conservation and flood control dams, pasture terraces and gully control work, and airports and runways. More visible, although requiring a smaller percentage of the total labor force, were public buildings, recreational facilities and cemetery improvements. Aside from sidewalks and culverts, these latter projects today are the ones most generally associated with the work of the WPA.

Symbolically and concretely, the significance of the WPA program in Oklahoma can hardly be overestimated. The public buildings, recreational facilities, and cemetery improvements suggest the economic importance of the total

WPA construction program in Northeastern Oklahoma. When employable persons had no jobs and faced the possibility of starvation, the WPA provided meaningful work and some financial security. The $31.20 per month paid unskilled workers was not much, but it was the margin between life and death. And it was just as important for the community collectively. Of the 51,292 monthly average number of WPA workers employed in Oklahoma between 1935 and 1941, some 35 percent, or almost 18,000, lived in the northeastern counties. Their collective salaries poured more than one half million dollars per month into local economies. This infusion unquestionably enabled many small retailers to stay in business when they would otherwise have gone under.

There was economic benefit beyond wage payments. In its public building program, the WPA utilized unskilled workmen as masons and carpenters. Over time they learned the crafts and at a later date entered the employed work force as skilled laborers. The evidence of this transition is still visible in Northeastern Oklahoma, where a large number of private houses and business buildings were constructed of native stone in WPA style. Of the overall economic impact of the program, the construction program prepared men to qualify as skilled and semi-skilled workmen. The morale of the workers was elevated due to their feeling that they had received training that increased their earning powers.

The program was also significant from a social/humanitarian perspective. In 1935 many county officials sincerely believed that the disposition of the people was such that insurrections and riots were seen as real possibilities. Local government officials were faced with starving, barefooted children and beleaguered residents who were depressed, bewildered, helpless, dependent, and at their wit's end. Some had lost their self-respect and were aimlessly walking the highways. The WPA program increased the morale of workers, renewed community spirit, gave people an opportunity to earn a living, and at the same time allowed them to maintain their self-respect. It was this intangible effect on the spirit that was the greatest value of the program.

The agency's massive employment program produced in the State at large 2,712 bridges and viaducts, 50,306 culverts, 585 miles of curbs, and 68 miles of gutter. Its laborers built 236 miles of malarial control ditches, 94,644 sanitary privies, and a whole host of water and sewage facilities. A fair number of all these were located in Northeastern Oklahoma. The largest percentage of WPA labor was assigned to the construction of these and similar projects. Most structures or facilities of these types have outlived their usefulness, except for some of the bridges and culverts along country roads and curbing and guttering in smaller communities.

The most lasting and obvious legacy of the program, however, was public buildings, recreational facilities, and cemetery improvements in Oklahoma's nineteen northeastern counties. They became major economic, social, educational, and cultural resources in the region. Construction of them eased economic distress, salvaged the self-esteem of destitute and unskilled workers, initiated an educational revival and reformation, enhanced the military preparedness of National Guard units that shortly afterward saw action in World War II, and gave expression to a distinct local architectural style recognizable by type, style, scale, materials, and workmanship. In summary, WPA-constructed public buildings, recreational facilities and cemetery improvements, although somewhat ordinary in appearance, possess extraordinary local historical architectural importance.

WPA public buildings and other improvements were of exceptional significance not only in Northeastern Oklahoma, but in the nation as a whole. The program changed the man-made landscape, provided economic security to thousands of destitute workers, helped preserve the economic vitality of local business communities, and produced social reforms still evident in the region. Put simply, from 1935 to 1941, the course of history in the area changed because of the WPA construction program.

Just as the overall WPA work program produced significant social and humanitarian benefits, so too did specific projects. The article that follows appeared on November 25, 1935, in the Hoffman High School journalism class newspaper, the Hoffman Herald.

GYMNASIUM PROJECT
by Helena Hood

A $11,000 building project began in Hoffman on November 6, 1935. Twenty-eight men are employed at the present time, ten more to be employed. When all are employed, fifty-six men will be working.

The building is to be 96 by 180 feet and 18 feet high. It is to be a combination auditorium and gymnasium and will also have two classrooms.

Mr. Eli Parker is the superintendent; Mr. Hubbard and Mr. Gallean are the stone masons.

The large building of native rock that was created by means of the project became the new Hoffman high school. The existing red brick building became the elementary school.

When the old red brick building burned down in 1941, a second native stone WPA-constructed school building was built in Hoffman. It became the new Hoffman Elementary School. When the WPA-built elementary school was itself burned down in yet another fire that occurred in later years, it was rebuilt by local businessman W. W. "Zant" Anthony. This building is still in use today, not as a school but as the home of the Hoffman Baptist Church.

It should also be mentioned that another WPA-funded project was the free lunch program offered by Hoffman School during the 1930s. The boys' dressing room in the high school was used as the lunchroom, and the meals of pinto beans, green split-pea soup, tomatoes, grapefruit, crackers, and butter were simple but nutritious. These meals were prepared by local men such as Sill Peters, Roy Painter, Joe Burney, Clarence Sessions, and William Jackson Tinny. High school girls helped to serve the meals.

Had there been no WPA school building and improvement projects in Okmulgee County during this period, it is likely that many school buildings would have been condemned and forced to close. The problem was that most school districts had reached the limit of their bonded indebtedness, making further issues impossible because assessed valuations of property had declined with the onset of the depression. The WPA school building program, therefore, was a Godsend to educational systems.

Not only were physical facilities improved, but new buildings inspired new interest in education and aided in the teaching process. School attendance in some rural districts increased markedly. For an area of high illiteracy, such developments were of great importance. Designed to admit light, to supply uncontaminated water, and to provide sanitary toilets, the new school buildings aided both learning and health. They enabled districts to attract and hold quality instructors. Put in other words, the WPA school buildings enabled the educational rebirth of Northeastern Oklahoma. The influence of the program remains in that in many locations the buildings are still in use today. Throughout Oklahoma 1,010 new schools were constructed during the life of the WPA, 12.5 percent of all those constructed nationwide. All other states but one (North Carolina) had less than one-half of the Oklahoma total.

Historical, Industrial and Civic

Survey of Okmulgee

and

Okmulgee County

Prepared for American Guide, WPA

Writers' Project

by

BAIRD MARTIN

Financed by Okmulgee Chamber of Commerce

Supervised by Okmulgee Daily Times

MAY 1936

Page 103 - Okmulgee

Government projects.

The federal works progress administration at the present

time (May 1936) has completed nine of its projects in Okmulgee

*LIST OF OKMULGEE COUNTY
WPA PROJECTS, PAGE 1*

Page 104 - Okmulgee

county and is pushing 36 others to completion.

Projects completed are (1) Construction of culverts on county roads and laying of bridges west of Beggs and west of Wilson; (2) extension of Okmulgee city water lines to out-lying sections of city; (3) cleaning channel of Deep Fork river; (4) re-copying county court probate docket; (5) extension of Henryetta sanitary sewers to Glendale addition; (6) laying shale sidewalks at Henryetta; (7) repairs and improvements to Dighton school; (8) repairs and improvements to Wilson rural school; (9) repairs and improvements to Dewar school; (10) construction of drainage ditch for Okmulgee creek.

Still operating are the following projects:

(1) Community sanitation including construction of concrete toilet units.

(2) Production of building stone.

(3) Construction of Beggs armory on Main street there, for Company E, 179th Infantry, Capt. E.E. Bettinger, commanding.

(4) Construction of Okmulgee armory at Third street and Alabama avenue for Company K, 179th Infantry, Capt. Elmer C. Croom commanding, and third battalion headquarters company, Lieut. Elmer A. Ward, commanding.

(5) Improvements to Henryetta waterworks and water lines.

(6) Changing channel of Wolf creek below dam at Lake Henryetta.

(7) Copying Okmulgee city records and statistics.

(8) Changing channel of Cedar Hollow creek at Henryetta.

LIST OF OKMULGEE COUNTY
WPA PROJECTS, PAGE 2

Page 105 - Okmulgee

(9) Construction of gymnasium-auditorium, Liberty school.

(10) Construction of new building at Hoffman school.

(11) Repairs and improvements to Preston school.

(12) Operation of sewing rooms.

(13) Construction of farm-to-market roads.

(14) Building of Okmulgee Harmon field stadium and grading of field.

(15) Repairs to Mayflower school.

(16) Repairs to Mountain View school.

(17) Construction of water standpipe at Okmulgee.

(18) Repairs at Pep school.

(19) Re-copying of Henryetta city records.

(20) Improvements to Morris city lake.

(21) Construction of corner setbacks on Okmulgee streets.

(22) Construction of new storm sewers in Okmulgee

(23) Filling abandoned mine shafts at and near Henryetta.

(24) Preparing school luncheons.

(25) Repairs to Henryetta water line.

(26) Construction of auditorium-gymnasium at Beggs.

(27) Repairs to Morris library books.

(28) Repairs to Okmulgee school library books.

(29) Work on county roads.

(30) Repairs and addition to Nuyaka school.

(31) Repairs to Radcliff school.

(32) Shaling Henryetta streets.

(33) Sponsoring Okmulgee county concert band.

(34) Repairs to Phillips school.

LIST OF OKMULGEE COUNTY
WPA PROJECTS, PAGE 3

HOFFMAN'S WPA-BUILT HIGH SCHOOL AND GYMNASIUM

NOTE: This picture was taken in September of 1972, years after the building had been abandoned. When it caught fire and burned some years later, locals salvaged the brick for building materials. No sign of the building remains.

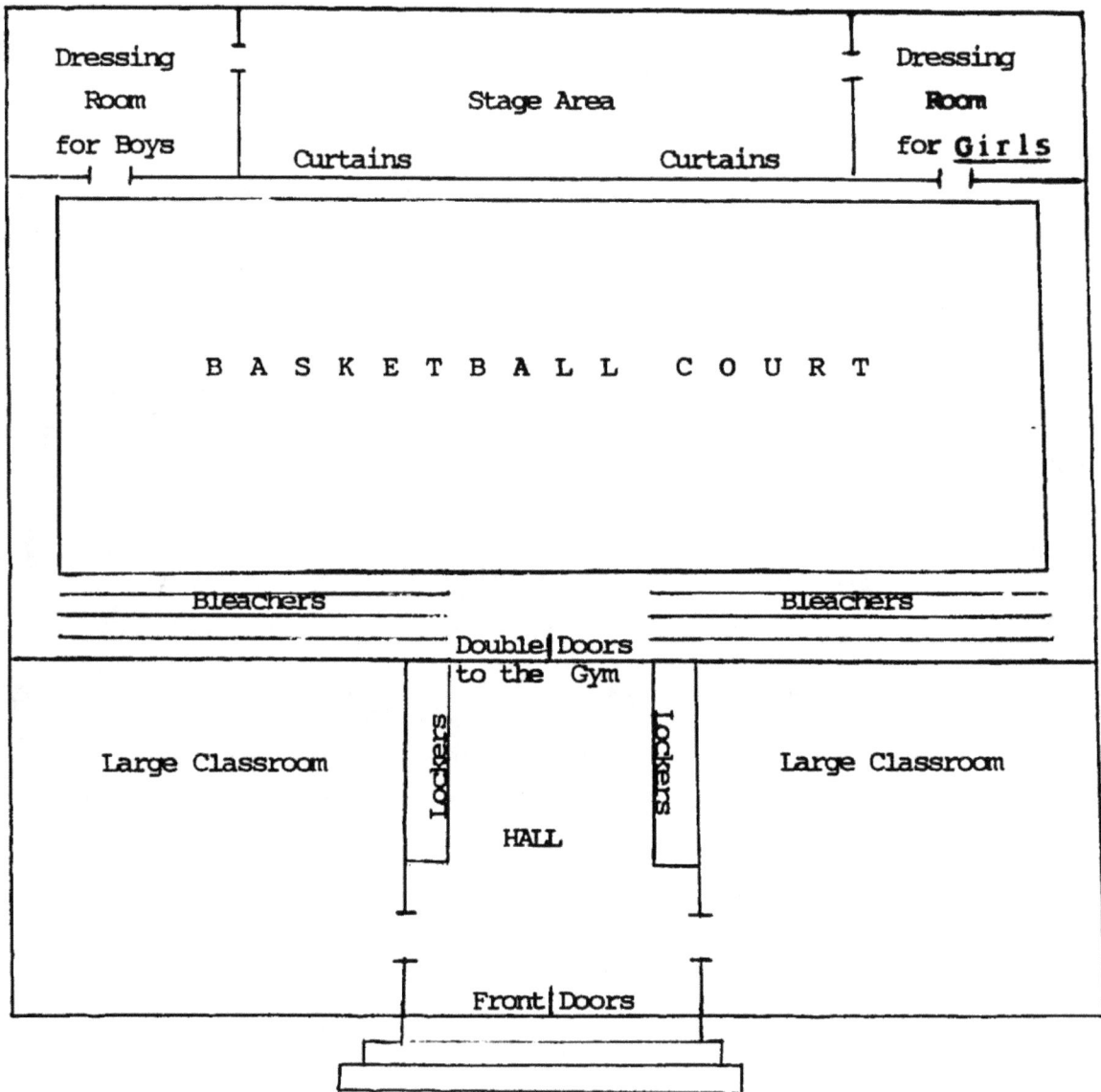

*FLOORPLAN OF THE HOFFMAN WPA HIGH
SCHOOL AND GYMNASIUM CONSTRUCTED IN 1935*

*Combination lunchroom-stage-classroom of Hoffman School's WPA-
Built High School and Gymnasium -- March 18, 1941*

Lunchroom Staff – March 18, 1941

Cleo Peters, National Youth Administration (NYA) helper
for teacher Kathleen Orendorff with first grade
students in the 1930s

Photograph taken in 1947 in front of Hoffman School's
WPA-built High School & Gymnasium

THE DUST BOWL PERIOD

At about the same time as the Great Depression, the Hoffman area was also caught up in what came to be called the "Dust Bowl" period of severe drought that so damaged the dry land farming areas across much of the United States during the 1930s. The problem was at its worst in the plains states from the Dakotas to Texas, but other areas, including parts of Oklahoma, were adversely affected as well. High and prolonged winds made drought conditions exceptionally severe. When water sources dried up, farm animals suffered and crops died in the fields. The effect was devastating on farmers and, in turn, on the farm laborers and small town merchants and professionals who indirectly depended on farm income for a living.

The dried out and unprotected topsoil on plowed land east of the hardest hit drought areas often created huge dust clouds that could be seen from many miles away. The wind also created generally miserable economic and living conditions. The Dust Bowl was centered in the panhandle areas of Texas and Oklahoma and in parts of Kansas, Colorado, and New Mexico, but peripheral areas such as Hoffman suffered as well. Wind erosion of topsoil caused by drought and unwise methods of land cultivation effectively forced many people off the land areas that were affected. Topsoil simply blew away, and with it went the means of thousands of people for making a living. Due to overproduction of farm goods and subsequent low farm prices during those times, farmers at all ends of the economic spectrum had trouble making a profit on their crops.

Even harder hit than small-town farmers and merchants were the sharecroppers, tenant farmers, and smaller independent farmers who had barely made a living in the best of times. Combined with the reduced need for labor and small farms brought on by agricultural mechanization, large numbers of people were forced to leave the Dust Bowl states to search for work. Because many of them were from Oklahoma, it was not long until "Okies" became a common collective term for all the Dustbowlers.

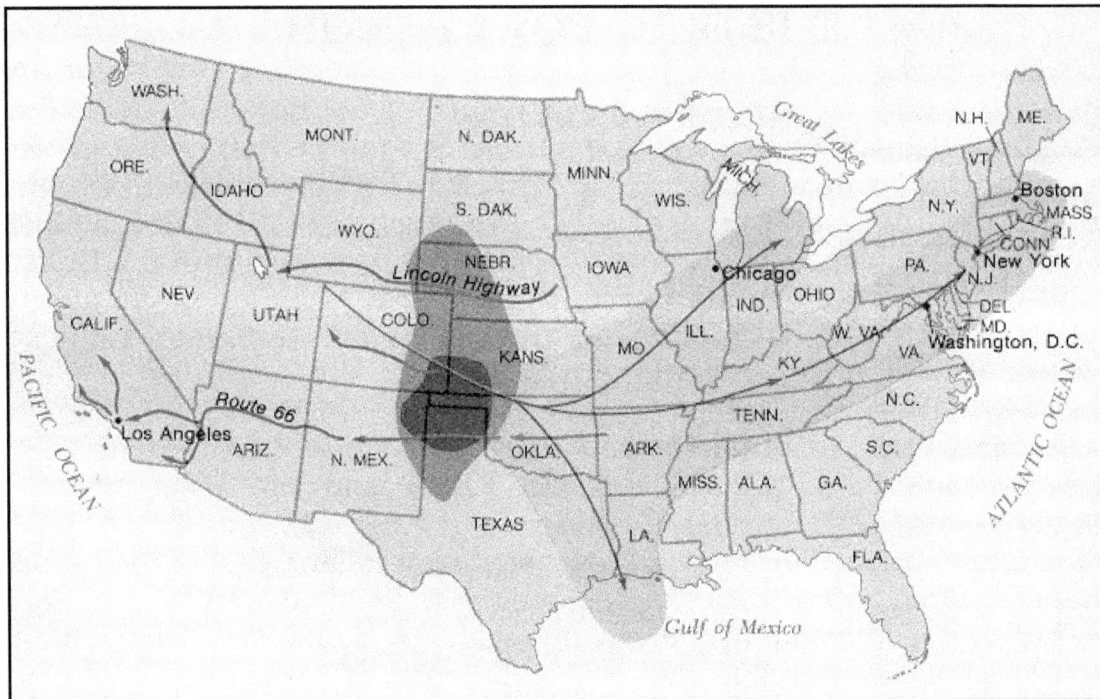

Overview of the Dust Bowl phenomenon of the 1930s. In a nutshell, the prevailing winds were toward the east while most of the out-migrating people went toward the west.

A rural Oklahoma farm of the 1930's. In 1935, this particular farm was owned by members of the Anthony family.

Hoffman Moves Ahead Despite Summer Drouth

HOFFMAN, Dec. 31. (Special) Despite the drouth and poor crop conditions, general advancement was made by Hoffman and surrounding country, a survey indicates. A number of public improvements were made during 1936.

Farmers here have an optimistic outlook and plan improvements for their land. Several farms have changed hands and will be operated by the new owners instead of by tenants.

At least one farm is to be converted into a modern dairy and another farmer plans to raise truck, using an irrigation system for the summer months if drouth conditions prevail again.

Although the pecan crop, one of the big money crops of this section, was a failure, a few thousand pounds were marketed here. Cotton ginned in the Hoffman plant amounted to 385 bales this year, far below the usual average.

Hoffman merchants, however, reported increased business, due to payrolls from governmental agencies and most business men look forward to a much better year in 1937.

The principal improvement made here during the year was the construction of a gymnasium-auditorium at the Hoffman school. This was built as a WPA project and, since its completion, is becoming a community center.

Roads in and around Hoffman have been greatly improved during the year and many highways have been brought to grade and drainage and new bridges and similar structures built.

Motor traffic through the town has been shown an increase. Hoffman is a mile. south of highway

———o———

*Daughter Lola (Tinney) Martin and nephew Phillip Charles Martin
at the family home of sharecropper William Jackson and
Cynthia Evline Tinney of Hoffman, around 1940*

William David "Dub" Martini in 1948

One of Hoffman's dry land Farmers, William David "Dub" Martin,
on his farm north of Hoffman

Sandy Martin, daughter of Robert and Mary Martin,
on her family's farm, also north of Hoffman

AGRICULTURAL MECHANIZATION

The economic viability of small farm towns like Hoffman was also undermined the industrialization of the country, specifically in the form of large-scale mechanized farming. Census figures for the 1920s showed that although the population of the United States had grown to 106 million people, for the first time in our national history more people were living in city areas than on farms in the country. Most still lived in very small cities, but it was clear that a significant shift in the kinds of work people were doing had taken place. More and more people were working in stores, factories, and service businesses than on farms--large or small.

By 1932, economic hardship around Hoffman was severe. In seven of the nineteen counties in the area, farm tax delinquencies reached a level of 70 percent. In all counties, relief rolls increased rapidly, a problem compounded by an in-migration of equally destitute people from the western counties of Oklahoma that had been even more directly hit by Dust Bowl conditions than Hoffman. By October 31, 1934, eight counties had 50 percent or more and seven had 20 to 49 percent of their local families on relief. In fact, 31 percent of all Oklahoma families on relief rolls were in the nineteen northeastern counties. By any economic measurement, the population of northeastern Oklahoma was in dire circumstances in 1935. It goes without saying that the spirit and morale of the people suffered as well.

THE CLOSING TIGER MOUNTAIN
SOUTH ROAD 300

The closure of north-west Road 300, which was referred to as "*the river road*" or "*Tiger Mountain Road*," from Hoffman across the Deep Fork River toward Tiger Mountain due to the construction of Lake Eufaula as a flood control project by Army Corps of Engineers was another blow to the farm and business economy in and around the town, in that it led to far fewer people traveling through the town. (In the first edition of this book, the closed road was mistakenly reported to be State Highway 266.) Other small farm towns in the area suffered in like manner. While the completion of east-west Interstate Highway 40 was an overall boon to the Sooner State, it further damaged Hoffman as an economic entity in and of itself. In addition, the convenience of the new interstate highway led to a marked decrease in the use of east-west Oklahoma State Highway 266, a highway that ran past the town about a mile to the north, which further reduced traffic through Hoffman.

LOSS OF ACCESS TO
PUBLIC SCHOOLING

Community life was strictly segregated in early Hoffman, just as it was in most every rural farm town in the South. Although its population by the late 1930s included about 250 whites and 150 blacks, a total of around 400 people, blacks were never fully integrated into the mainstream of town society. Racial segregation was not directly spoken about in those days as it is now, but it was clearly "understood" that the races were not to mix on equal terms in schools, churches, restaurants, barbershops, transportation services, theaters, and so on.

The white population lived mainly on the north side of town while blacks, called "Coloreds," lived on the south side in what was commonly called "Niggertown." (Blacks of the time, it should be noted, used equally thoughtless and condescending terms--now, thankfully, largely outgrown--for the white community.) The local Creek Indian population probably used even more colorful expressions to refer to the white and black races--collectively and separately. At the very least, it is fair to say that the bigotry and ignorance that existed in those days--and there was more than just a little--was fairly equally distributed, pretty much just like it is today.

All three populations engaged in farming in plots surrounding the town and traded in the same stores. Even though the pecking order of the day clearly made second-class citizens of the black population, many whites were not much better off economically than the blacks or Indians and, since most people had grown up with the system, relations among the races was generally friendly and cooperative. Most people in the area during the period between 1905 and the late 1920s thought of and referred to Hoffman as "a nice little town in which to live, start a business or farm, and raise a family."

Whatever its benefits might have been, segregation was never an inexpensive proposition. The maintenance of separate schools for blacks and whites--and, in some cases, Indians--was a costly burden for small towns like Hoffman. It has been said that the soul of Hoffman truly began to wither and die when the high school closed at the end of the 1940-41 school year. The final death blow, however, came years later when the elementary school was disbanded and its students and physical assets were divided up among the neighboring Morris, Schulter, and Dewar School Districts in 1968. Many of the local residents actually preferred to see the local school shut down than to bow to forced integration.

Without convenient access to a school for their children, even more families moved out of town and new families could not be drawn to the area to replace them. According to student census and enrollment reports sent to the State of Oklahoma by the Okmulgee County Schools, when the Hoffman and Grayson elementary schools closed at the end of the 1967-68 school year there were just 78 families living in the Hoffman school district. There were 84 male and 102 female students, or a total of 186 children. Just one year before there had been a total of 97 families and 193 students.

CLASS PICTURE IN THE 1930'S

Note that some students are barefooted and wearing flower sack clothing.

~les Geor~

AUNT SAMANTHY RULES THE ROOST

By Charles George

HOFFMAN JUNIOR PLAY
Friday Night April 26, 1940

Time - 7:30

Characters:

Aunt Samanthy Simpkins---Darlene Wadsworth----An old Maid.

Serena Simpkins----------Wilma Jean Farrell---Her older niece.

Sophie Simpkins----------Eunice Smith---------Her younger niece.

Polly Paine--------------Wanda Palmer---------Maid at the Simpkins'

Annie Ambrose------------Joyce Bowden---------Village dressmaker.

Blanche Bowers-----------Billye June Peters---A woman of few words.

Lucien Littlefield-------Garland McCarty------A farmer.

Blair Boswell-----------Luther Conklin-------Who likes Serena.

Frank Fairfield----------A. C. Hyatt---------Who likes Sophie.

Lawrence Lovewell-------Lee Christenberry-----A stranger.

Buddy Baskins-----------Junior Hamilton-------The grocery boy

Time - The present

Place - Home of Samanthy Simpkins in Simpkinsville

Time of Playing - Two Hours and Fifteen Minutes

ADMISSION : Adults - 15¢

Children - 10¢

HOFFMAN SCHOOL PLAYBILL
APRIL 26, 1940

TOP: Cast of Hoffman High School play "Aunt Samanthy Rules the Roost". BOTTOM LEFT: Teacher-Principal Willie G. Smith or Bliss Pannell. BOTTOM RIGHT: Teacher-Principal Ted Smith, last administrative employee at Hoffman School.

HOFFMAN HIGH SCHOOL CLASS OF 1941

LAST GRADUATES OF HOFFMAN HIGH SCHOOL

Eunice Smith, Emma Lee Milam, Pricilla Christenberry, Wanda Jean Palmer, Leroy Christenberry, A. C. "Jim" Hyatt, Elmer Robnett, Billye June Peters, George "Ham" Hamilton, Jr., and Teacher Howard L. Smith

THE DEATH OF BUSINESSMAN
CHARLEY E. LACKEY

As unquantifiable in effect as it may have been, the death of C. E. Lackey was a strictly local event that had a definite economic impact on the health of Hoffman Townsite. Charley E. Lackey was one of Hoffman's most prominent businessmen. In fact, some thought that Charley Lackey *was* Hoffman. As the owner of business properties and a good deal of leasable farm land, a blacksmith's shop, a butcher's shop (operated out of his store), a slaughter house (located one block from the store), a feed business, and the Charley E. Lackey General Store, he and his wife Stella were among the town's most prosperous citizens--wealthy enough, for example, to own an airplane in days when many were barely making a living. (Another Lackey, Sanford, was said to "own" the neighboring town of Hitchita in the same way that Charley "owned" Hoffman.) It was also said that Charley made additional income by carrying the costs (for a fee) of the furnishings and supplies needed by local men willing to accept the risk of making bootleg whiskey, then buying the finished product at a bargain price to sell under the counter out of his own store.

For many years the highly respected and successful Mr. Lackey had either rented or leased farmland and provided credit for seed, groceries, and other necessities of life, usually both, to local sharecroppers and tenant farmers, especially among the black population. Just a few of those who farmed land he owned were Sherman Howk, Charley Stanton, Bud Owens, Bill Childs, and William Jackson Tinny. With the local economy heavily reliant on this mode of farming, when no one of his stature, reputation, and general business acumen stepped in to replace him when he was accidentally killed by a gunshot, many of the local farmers, black and white, gradually began to move away. As they left, local businesses and services of other kinds struggled to survive and they, too, eventually began to shut down.

The gunshot incident that so affected Hoffman occurred in August 15, 1943, and it took place in Lackey's own store at the corner of Main and Broadway Streets right in the center of Hoffman. It happened when Preacher Porter and Charley's own store clerk, Tom Knight, got into an argument over something that today no one seems to remember, even though a number of witnesses, both blacks and whites, were said to be present when it happened.

John Henry Porter, or "Preacher Porter," as he was called back then, was pastor of the local Assembly of God Church. (Some say it was the Pentecostal Holiness Church; recollections differ.) He had epilepsy, and, in a time when this affliction was not as well understood as it is today, he suffered from periodic unexpected seizures. Like many of the essentially self-educated preachers of his time, he was not much different from most of his flock in terms of temperament and fundamental beliefs. Some thought him to be a pretender, but most considered him to be a hellfire and brimstone preacher who "knew his Bible backwards and forwards." At times, however, he could become a bit assertive and overly zealous, and there were days when he would go straight from his church with collection plate money to mingle with and to try to convert the local men who drank and shot dice down by the town jail. When he was in this frame of mind, he could sometimes be rather contentious.

Tom Knight was a farmer who also worked as the clerk of Lackey's general store on Main Street. A tall, lean, rawboned man who lived over by Hoffman School not too far from the store, he was considered to be something of a grumpy old man because he lived alone in the old T. C. Cole house. Some of the young boys of Hoffman were a little afraid of him due to his general disposition and what were viewed as some strange personal practices. Basically, they considered him to be mean and cranky. For example, each Halloween he would sit at the front of his home with a shotgun across his lap to prevent trick-or-treaters from knocking over his outhouse. (They usually found a way to tip it over anyway!) He was also considered somewhat mysterious because when someone got cut he would read a verse out of the Bible to stop the bleeding. And once after Dempsey Martin, Robert Martin, and Jack Ray had picked cotton one day on his farm, Knight refused to pay Dempsey for his work. George Martin, Dempsey's father, threatened, so the story goes, to "beat the hell" out of him before he would agree to pay the wages he had promised. When he passed away some years later, no one knew how to contact any members of his family.

Somehow the combative disposition and temper these two men were capable of displaying under the right combination of circumstances got out of control on that particular day, and their interaction turned into a bitter and heated argument that finally got the better of Tom Knight. When he lunged to pull a gun from behind the store counter and tried to shoot the Preacher, Charley Lackey jumped between them just in time to deflect the shot. Instead, Knight's bullet struck Lackey himself, entering his leg just above the knee. Though Pierce Burney and Bill Phillips immediately took him to a doctor in Henryetta, the bullet had hit an artery and Charley bled to death before anything could be done to save him. He was gone before the day was over, and today his remains are at rest in the Lackey family cemetery about a mile off the road toward Hitchita.

The death of Charley E. Lackey was considered by many to be perhaps the final nail in Hoffman's coffin in terms of its viability as a local center of economic activity. The day he died, George Martin, a long-term resident of Hoffman, predicted that "this will be the end of Hoffman." As it turned out, he was at least partly right. Lackey's death turned out to be one of the final links in the chain of events that helped push the town and the surrounding area into decline. Charley's son, Charles, or "Little Charles," as he was called back then, took over the family businesses for a while, but he was not able to sustain the level of activity his father had reached during more prosperous economic times. After a while, he too moved out of Hoffman.

Businessman Charlie E. Lackey

STRUCTURAL FIRES
AND THE TORNADO OF 1960

Even as businesses and offices continued to close over the years, major fires in 1929 and 1940 and several smaller fires destroyed many of the store buildings in Hoffman. Wanda Bowden and other residents recall sadly and helplessly watching as the big fire of April 9, 1940, destroyed most of the business buildings once located on the northwest corner block of the intersection of Main and Broadway Streets. With generally slow and unreliable fire protection, once the dried-out wood frames of the old buildings caught on fire it was almost impossible to save them.

And as if to add to Hoffman's list of woes, on May 1, 1960, the town was struck by a powerful tornado. Many buildings that had stood in Hoffman for over 60 years were torn to pieces in a few frightful seconds. According to newspaper reports, the tornado hit with all the force and destructiveness of a runaway freight train, dipping down out of a bright and clear spring sky to cut a broad swath through town that stayed visible for years thereafter.

Many former residents of Hoffman remember the tornado with painful clarity. The wind had come up and large hail stones had pelted the area, then things became eerily quiet. Although the sun had started shining bright and the air was still, suddenly and without warning a tremendous rushing noise was heard. From the southwest, a huge greenish-black cloud pressed down out of the sky towards the town. The tornado struck many of the town's small wood frame houses with enough force to almost instantly tear them into pieces or tear them off their foundations. A number of families lost all they owned in just a few seconds.

Despite generous relief assistance from the Red Cross, the tornado of May 1, 1960, became just another calamity in the series of economic disasters to strike Hoffman since the 1930s. Most of the business buildings destroyed by the tornado were never replaced, further increasing the level of local economic distress.

THE BITTER END

Although Hoffman did indeed benefit from many of the New Deal programs enacted by the Roosevelt administration of the Thirties, the combined effects of the Depression and the Dust Bowl years had a severely adverse economic impact on the townsite. Essentially a dry land farming area, it was effectively crushed by these two major historical events--especially when combined with the effect of additional blows such as the impact of agricultural mechanization, the closing of one of the major State highways that served the area, the death or departure of leading business figures such as Charley Lackey, and natural disasters such as fires and tornados.

Beginning in the 1930s, Hoffman began to slowly fade away as a viable townsite. Its fate was like that of many small farm towns of its kind. Without industry or enough farm employment to provide dependable job opportunities, even those who would have preferred to stay in the area could not afford to do so. Very simply, economic stagnation forced many to move away in search of better ways to make a living, giving rise, at least in part, to the Okie migration of the 1930s through the early 1950s.

*Aerial view of damage caused
by the Tornado of May 1, 1960*

*Tornado destroyed home of the
Buster Ivory family -- May 1, 1960*

*Tornado damage in the black section
of Hoffman -- May 1, 1960*

*Tornado destroyed home of the England family in May of 1960.
The family was trapped under this debris. The man sifting
through the ruins is Clarence Dodson.*

CHAPTER VI

THE OKIE MIGRATION

In the mid-Thirties, prospects for getting ahead in the world seemed hopelessly bleak to many people, especially so to those living in isolated country towns. Hoffman, for example, was a tiny farm community located within a mile of the Deep Fork River, surrounded by wooded lands on the south and west and prairie lands on the north and east. It was about one mile from the nearest paved road, Oklahoma State Highway 266. The major farm output was cotton, corn, and livestock. It was a pecan market center, and there was some limited production of oil, gas, minerals, and native lumber. It had a population of about 350 people, and there were two public schools (one for blacks and one for whites), four churches (two for whites and two for blacks), one hotel, and one Woman's Home Demonstration Club. Opportunity was so lacking that it was no wonder when some people almost starved during this period of time, nor was it a surprise to anyone when men started to leave the area in search of work.

The Hoffman Herald (not to be confused with the commercial newspaper of the early 1900s) was a newspaper published as a project of the Hoffman High School journalism class of 1935-36. It was to be produced every two weeks "in the interest of the entire student body" by the following students and staff:

Editor	Wilford Duncan
Society Editor	Helena Hood
Humor Editor	Ruby McFarlin
Sports Editor	Brunell Lackey
Advertising Manager	Kalman Anthony
Circulation Manager	Ralph Rains
Reporters	Marie Rains, Alma Leah Hunter, Jewell Prevett, Dorothy Duncan, Louise Hamilton, and Hazel Browning
Typist	Miss Laura Blake
Staff Director	Ulys M. Morgan

The Herald was published for only that one year. In fact, it is likely that only a few issues (and perhaps only this one) were ever published.

On November 25, 1935, Helena Hood, Society Editor of the Herald, wrote the following article for the paper:

CALIFORNIA CRAZY
by Helena Hood

Several of our friends have gone to California in search of work and vari-ous other reasons. Those who have gone are Stella Hooper, Edgar Bundy, Arval Edwards, Carney Ritterhoff and Hobart Johnson. Edgar Bundy has returned from his trip. The others seem to like California quite well.

California became a common destination of Okies at the lower end of the socioeconomic spectrum, where many had heard that they could find field and orchard work during those difficult economic times. First leaving on exploratory trips that were temporary in length, the rate of migration later increased from a trickle to a flood. Over a period of years, whole families migrated from small farm towns in Oklahoma to find a fresh start in California. Those who owned a car or truck packed as much of their belongings as they could carry and headed out on the westward highway, often to an only generally known destination. Others hitchhiked, jumped on railroad boxcars, or teamed up with friends to make their trip.

With little if any money, no dependable contacts, and only the shakiest prospects for improving their lot in life, families began to leave their little farm towns, their friends, and the only way of living they had ever known. Most were almost destitute, and many had to camp along the way wherever they could find the basic requirements of a usable campsite--a source of water and a place to throw out some blankets or pitch a tent for the night. Firewood was scavenged wherever it could be found. Mothers had to get used to cooking over a campfire and caring for their children on roadsides or riverbanks. With little money to live on and even less to spend on repairs, those who made the trip by car were always fearful of a serious mechanical breakdown such as an engine or transmission problem. Flat tires and overheated radiators were common in the almost always already rundown cars and trucks in which many of these families traveled.

What most did not imagine is that by leaving their farm communities and their roles as farmers they were also, by default, changing their very status in life. They became not ex-farmers or even ex-farm laborers, but migrant workers. For their entire lives, some were deeply affected by events that would occur as consequences of their move. Some were never able to break out of the mindset formed by the stress, disorientation, and even trauma experienced as they left behind the kind of life they had grown used to living. Once concerned only with farm work and hunting and fishing, they had to face the blunt reality of having to make new places for themselves in new areas where they were not always as welcome as they had hoped to be. In some cases, their experiences were harsh and difficult.

The Martin family was typical of many that began to make exploratory trips from Hoffman to California in those days in search of seasonal work, in the fields, permanent economic opportunity, or, in some cases, a little adventure. One of their early trips out west occurred in the summer of 1939. The travelers were headed by George Jackson Martin and his wife, Virginia Victoria (McFarland) Martin, and they were more fortunate than many that made similar trips back then--they were able to travel in a new 1939 Chevrolet half-ton pickup Mr. Martin had bought for $600 on a time payment plan landed with the help of loan officer Peyster of the Morris State Bank and a down payment scraped together by selling hogs, hauling cotton seed, and doing odd jobs. The truck was his only possession.

Some of the money put together to finance the new truck and the trip out west was provided by Mr. Martin's sons, inasmuch as any wages they earned were automatically turned over to their father instead of being kept by themselves. Their father decided when they were to have any spending money. Up until the time his sons were married and had homes of their own, this was common practice in the Martin household. In those days, it made economic sense for a man to have a lot of sons!

Having lived in Hoffman for almost all their lives, everyone in the Martin family knew by first name everyone else in town. Several of their neighbors had heard about their trip and had either asked or were invited to go along. By the day of the departure, fourteen people were ready to be loaded on the truck. Among those who made the trip on that date were George, Virginia, William David (or Dub), Lola (Tinny), Charlie, Robert, Dempsey, Naomi, and George (Sonny) Martin, Joyce Bean, Mary Lou and Jimmy Hart, and Dub Martin's dog. Their number made for quite a cozy journey.

Finally, on a hot July day in 1939, the group pulled out of Hoffman and headed out for California. Feeling excited and happy (and, probably, a little tentative and nervous), everyone was pleased to be on the road. George's eldest son, Dub, did most of the driving, his mother and father riding aside him on the front seat. All other members of the group rode in the bed of the truck, on padding made of blankets. One night of the trip they slept in a cabin near a bubbling stream near St. John's, Arizona, but most of the time they camped by the highway, sleeping in the truck or on blankets spread on the ground. A temporary top had been built to enclose the truck bed as a shelter (it looked like a big box), and a wooden ladder had been added as a means of getting to its top. Meals of beans and potatoes in the evenings and flapjacks in the mornings were cooked over a campfire, and water was drawn from rivers or service stations faucets.

The trip to California took over a month. The travelers got lost and hungry several times along the way, and they had to hold up in Flagstaff, Arizona, when they were delayed by a creek flood. When they almost ran out of food before the water went down, Mary Lou bought a five-pound box of cheese and crackers that everyone shared later during the trip. When money ran out a few days later, they worked for several weeks in T. G. "Snow" Anthony's logging camp to earn enough to get back on the road again. Snow, like the travelers, was also a former Hoffmanite, who was operating a sawmill on government-owned land under a contract that permitted him to cut out diseased and fallen timber for forest protection. During the stay in Arizona, the children remembered killing a large rattlesnake and watching forest station rangers break horses in corral near their campsite.

Eventually, the members of the group who had not stayed in Arizona arrived in Riverbank, a farm town in the center of California's San Joaquin Valley. Shortly after their arrival, they went to work in the orchards that were located around Riverbank in those days just as they are today. Early during their stay, they picked peaches at a pay rate of "5¢ per 48-pound box for the good ones and 3¢ per box for the bad ones." Later, some landed jobs at the Darpenian Dry Yard, where their rate of pay jumped to 15¢ per hour. After signing up for "social security" cards to take advantage of one of the Roosevelt administration's new anti-depression programs, members of the group felt they were truly on the way to stability and success. When the work ran out around Riverbank, they traveled to other Valley towns such as Arvin, Poplar, and Porterville to find another field or orchard in which to work.

Some native Californians considered even the honest and law-abiding "Okies" suspect and unwelcome during those tough economic times. Once in 1940, for example, on the outskirts of the town of Porterville, George, William (or "Dub"), Walker, Charlie, Robert, and Dempsey Martin pulled off a main road into an orchard to ask a grower by the name of Cantrell for work. Jumping to the conclusion that the family was a group of strikers, the grower immediately shot at them with a high-powered deer rifle. One bullet went through the front windshield of the 1939 Chevrolet pickup the men were in, badly wounding Dub's face with fragments of flying glass. After tearing away from the orchard as fast as they could in their panic, the irate family returned with police officers to have the rancher arrested for assault. Cantrell was taken to court, but he was given no jail time even though he had almost killed a man without justification. The incident was reported in an article in the Porterville Times.

As if the problems caused by the depression were not enough, Hoffman was also caught up in the period of severe drought that so damaged dry land farming areas across much of the United States during the 1930s. The problem was at its worst in plains states from the Dakotas to Texas, the region of the country where high and prolonged winds made drought conditions exceptionally severe. Water sources dried up, farm animals suffered, and crops died in the fields. The effect on farmers and, in turn, on the farm laborers and small-town merchants who depended on farm income, was devastating.

Persistently strong winds blew dried out and unprotected topsoil on plowed land towards the east, often creating huge dust clouds that could be seen from many miles away. The wind also created generally miserable economic and living conditions. The so-called "Dust Bowl" was centered in the panhandle areas of Texas and Oklahoma and in parts of Kansas, Colorado, and New Mexico, but peripheral areas suffered as well. Wind erosion of topsoil caused by drought and unwise methods of land cultivation, in effect, forced many people off the land areas that were affected. Topsoil simply blew away, and with it went thousands of people who had depended on it for a living. Due to aggregate overproduction of farm goods and subsequent low farm prices during those times, farmers at all ends of the economic spectrum had trouble making a profit on their crops.

Even harder hit than farmers and merchants were sharecroppers, tenant farmers, and smaller independent farmers, people who had had trouble making a living even in the best of times. Combined with a reduced need for labor and small farms brought on by agricultural mechanization, large numbers of people were forced to leave the Dust Bowl states in search for work. Because many of them were from Oklahoma, it was not long until "Okies" became the common collective term for all Dustbowlers.

Most of the members of the Martin family group who traveled to California worked hard and played hard, but after about four months they had saved enough money to return to their hometown of Hoffman. While they did indeed return, for many a die had been cast; the old home place never looked the same after their first exploratory and short-termed trip out west to find the temporary work they needed to get by. In the years that followed, many of the younger men and women left Oklahoma again—often never to permanently return.

Influenced by the departure of their friends and members of their own extended family, one by one the young men of the Martin family began to pull up stakes and move out west. As one family gained an economic toehold in California, others would make periodic trips out there to work or just to keep in touch with their loved ones. The Martin brothers, for example, were especially close in those days, and some of the brothers who first stayed on in Hoffman soon began to look forward to occasions such as the Christmas holidays when vacation time was available for a visit of several weeks with family and friends who had moved out west.

Charlie Martin, George Martin's second oldest son, who married Evie Edwards, daughter of Charley and Vada Anna Adeline (Winkenplex or Winkempleck) Edwards, was one of the first to move to California for good. Once there he moved around for a time doing various kinds of field work, but he eventually settled in the town of Oakdale in the San Joaquin Valley to put down permanent roots. After a time, he opened his own combination service station, garage, restaurant, and bar business, then built a home on a lot he purchased on the outskirts of town. Charlie and Evie had three sons of their own--Charles, David, and Bruce. David died as a young child, but the other two boys still live in the central San Joaquin Valley.

When his younger brother Robert, George Martin's third oldest son, who married another daughter of Charley and Vada Anna Adeline (Winkenplex or Winkempleck) Edwards, visited with him during that period of time, Charley's relative success and the general sense of optimism he projected had a tremendous impact on the way Robert saw his life in Hoffman. If brother Charlie could do so well in California, Robert began to believe that he might be able do the same. After unsuccessfully struggling for years to get ahead by working a fulltime county job, tending to a eighty-acre dry land farm, and taking agricultural extension in the evenings, it was not long before Robert, like his brother before him, was ready to try something new.

For years, however, Robert hesitated to leave the home of his youth and the place he loved for an uncertain future in a new state. As time passed, his family grew to seven children--Mickey, Dickey, Bobby, Tony, Sandy, Tommy, and Ronny. (They later had two more children, Susan and Judy, but their son Ronny died when he was six months old and was buried in the Hoffman Cemetery.) With only sporadic school attendance up to the eighth-grade level and limited specific skills to sell in the job market, his reluctance to leave Hoffman was certainly not unfounded. Among the jobs he had done early in life, for example, were picking cotton and helping his Uncle Alvis, a local trapper, skin game animals. His role in the latter occupation had been to hold the animals while his Uncle skinned them for their meat and fur. His Uncle Alvis sold the hides, but he gave the skinned carcasses to young Robert to sell for cash by carrying them door to door in the black section of Hoffman.

Not needing to be told that picking cotton and animal skinning were unlikely to be viewed as high demand occupations in California, it was only after years of hesitation that Robert finally made his decision to follow his older and more daring brother Charlie out west. One summer evening after a hot day of work driving a county road grader, he surprised his oldest son, Mickey, about seven years old at the time, by asking with feigned seriousness "What do you think, Mick; should we pack up and move to California?" After a moment of hesitation in which he recalled some recent happy Christmas vacations enjoyed with his cousins, Charles and Bruce, in the home of his relatively prosperous Uncle Charlie out west, Mickey swallowed hard and answered: *"I think we should do it!"* With that discussion, another member of the Martin family of Hoffman, Oklahoma, decided to migrate to California. Eventually, George Martin's entire family--and George himself--were rejoined as a family in the Golden State.

It was in 1954 that Robert and his wife Mary and the first six of their nine children loaded their belongings into a 1950 Chevrolet sedan to make their final trip from Hoffman to the "Promised Land." Their first stay was on the outskirts of Porterville, California, at a place called Hood's Camp. Hood's Camp was a small cluster of 10' X 18' farm labor cabins, a grocery store, a garage, a small car lot, and a communal shower and restroom facility (featuring the first residential flush toilet the Martin's had ever had access to) owned and operated by Hobert and Ortha Hood.

Robert and Mary loaded up their children and left the camp each day to do farm labor piece work such as picking or hoeing cotton, cutting lemons, picking or swamping peaches, or cleaning fields of pie melons. The family struggled through many hard years of barely making a living as farm laborers, and it is easy to imagine how Robert must have longed for the good old days of his carefree youth back in his little hometown of Hoffman.

Eventually, however, Robert landed a permanent job and was able to buy a home for his family. It wasn't easy, but he was able to get all of his children through high school and to see them happily married and self-sufficient. In addition, he was able to build a good retirement for himself and his wife Mary. Today, he travels from California back to Hoffman twice each year for long vacations of hunting and fishing along the shores of Lake Eufaula. He has never forgotten the friends of his youth, and there is no place in the country he enjoys more than the lakes and river bottoms around his hometown--Hoffman, Oklahoma.

With many different variations, this same chain of events was repeated by family after family in the poverty-stricken areas of states such as Oklahoma in the years that followed the Great Depression and the Dust Bowl. Some students of the subject have estimated that as many as 1 million ex-farm workers from that region of the country ultimately wound up in California, where--at least during the early period of their lives there--their economic situation was in many cases actually worsened rather than improved.

Happily, most of the migrants, like Charlie and Evie and Robert and Mary Martin, did indeed go on to build better lives for themselves in California, just as they had hoped. Today, their children and children's children are just as likely as anyone else's to be the teachers, engineers, policemen, and so on that make up the working population of the state. For them, the American Dream did, in fact, become a reality.

Robert Martin with his children Mickey, Dickey, Bobby, Sandy (in her father's arms), and Tony and the boys' dog Skipper at his rental farm north of Hoffman

Members of the Edwards and Parker families on the road to California in April of 1943. Pictured are Irene Parker (with the camera), Vada (Winkemplex) Edwards, Dorothy (Porter) Edwards, Bill Edwards (back to the camera), Charlie Edwards, Bessie Edwards, and Pirley May Edwards. Bill Edwards' shaving pan and mirror can be seen in the background.
NOTE: This photograph was taken in Arizona, in the desert near Winslow.

Hood's Camp in Porterville, California, a private farm labor camp. This photograph was taken during the Tule River flood of 1943. The two-room cabins at the camp measured 10' x 18'.

Hobert and Ortha Hood, Owner-Managers of Hood's Camp.

FAMILY OF GEORGE JACKSON MARTIN
AT HOOD'S CAMP IN PORTERVILLE, CALIFORNIA, IN 1943

TOP: George Jackson Martin, Virginia Martin, Robert "Bob" Martin (arm over his mother's shoulder), Charlie Martin (in uniform), Eva "Evie" Martin, William David "Dub" Martin, and an Unknown Navy buddy of Charlie's. BOTTOM: Dempsey, George "Sonny," and Naomi Martin.

Brothers Charlie R. (left) and Robert J. Martin of Hoffman, Oklahoma.
The brothers married sisters Eva (left) and Mary Edwards, also of
Hoffman. This picture was taken in the early 1940's.

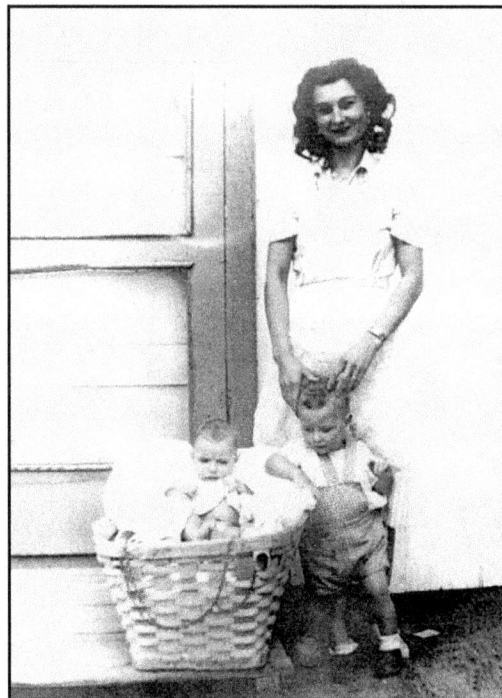

TOP LEFT: Francis Blunt, age 9, in front of a cabin at Hood's Camp in Porterville, California. TOP RIGHT: Mary (Edwards) Martin at Hood's Camp. BOTTOM: Robert and Mary Martin's children Dickey, Tony, Mickey, Bobby, cousin Bruce and grandmother Virginia Victoria (McFarlin) Martin at Hood's Camp.

Christmas visit of the Robert Martin Family of Hoffman, Oklahoma, with the family of Charlie Martin and his wife Eva of California. At the Time, Charlie owned and managed a combination bar, grill, service station and garage that was referred to as The Orange Blossom Station. It was located near Oakdale, California. Pictured below are Dickey Martin, Bruce Martin, unknown baby, grandmother Virginia Victoria (McFarlin) Martin, unknown baby, Sandy Martin (squatting down), Bobby Martin, Tony Martin (squatting down), and Mickey "Mike" Martin.

Charlie Martin at Martin's Norwalk Service, which was located
near Oakdale, California. It was referred to as
The Orange Blossom Station.

*Lola (Tinney) Martin, Picking Peaches
near Oakdale, California*

*Dick Martin, picking peaches
near Riverbank, California*

CHILDREN OF ROBERT AND MARY MARTIN
OF HOFFMAN, OKLAHOMA
*From L. to R.: Mickey, Dickey, Bobby, Tony, Sandy,
Ronny (deceased), Tommy, Susan and Judy*

RONNY EUGENE MARTIN
"Always Remembered!"

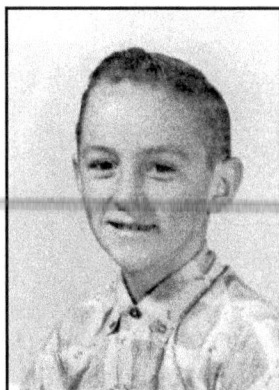

CHILDREN OF CHARLIE AND EVA "EVIE" MARTIN
OF HOFFMAN, OKLAHOMA

TOP LEFT: Charles and Bruce Martin. TOP RIGHT:
Phillip Charles "Chuck" or "Slug" Martin. BOTTOM CENTER:
David Martin, deceased but always remembered.

CHAPTER VII

DEATH
OF THE TOWNSITE

On April 12, 1966, at 2:00 p.m., citizens of Hoffman who had not moved away held a town meeting to vote on a single question: *"Shall the Corporation of the Town of Hoffman be dissolved?"* Sixty-two residents turned out for the vote, more than two-fifths of the town's registered voters. Of those who were present, over two-thirds voted in favor of the petition--43 "Yes" against 19 "No"--and on October 12, 1966, six months after the date of the vote, the waiting period required by the laws of the State of Oklahoma, the Okmulgee County farm town of Hoffman was legally dissolved and officially ceased to be. It had been in existence a total of 61 years, 11 months, and 15 days.

Having been forced to come to grips with the blunt economic reality of a tax base too small to support such basic necessities of town life as an adequate water system, street maintenance, fire protection, and law enforcement, Hoffman's struggling citizens had felt compelled to petition for the town meeting to consider the dissolution of the Township Corporation. With little or no prospects of better economic conditions in sight, few were able or willing to continue trying to kick a dead horse back to life.

Due to having been beaten down by a devastating combination of natural and economic disasters, homes and businesses were not rebuilt and many once productive small farms were, at least for a time, allowed to revert to a natural state. It was a bitterly difficult time, especially for those who were bound to the place by memories of better days, back when they had gone to school, met their first sweethearts, gotten married, raised their children, built a home or business or farm, and experienced all the many other daily occurrences that combine to constitute a lifetime.

Today, as the last visible remnants of the old Hoffman townsite continue to slowly fade from existence, it is a shame to think that most future visitors will look on what remains of the little town and strip away its significance and meaning by saying, in effect, "It did not matter." In the same way that the media often caricatured American Indians and their relationship with our country's early settlers, those who take only a casual look at Oklahoma's townsite days will leave only partially informed or, in some instances, totally misinformed with regard to the way average people lived back then.

In the absence of accounts like this one that depict what life at Hoffman was really like, it, too, would stay incompletely or inaccurately understood. Without a record of this kind, fact and fiction too easily become intermixed and the true story becomes blurred, making it unnecessarily difficult to learn from what happened there and hard to apply understanding of the place to help us more effectively deal with the social and moral issues of our lives today. Fictitious stories about times there can be entertaining, but such stories are not as helpful in terms of meeting current challenges as the unvarnished truth. Hoffman was not simply a dream or an accidental event; it was an historical episode in which men and women acted out their lives just as they do today. Some of the values on which they based their lives are more than worthy of emulation, and we can learn a great deal by carefully considering their successes as well as their mistakes.

Many small townsites of 100 years ago were devastated when our nation went through a relatively rapid transition from an agricultural to an industrial economy. By studying the experience of Hoffman and other townsites like it, we may gain insights that can help us deal with transitions going on today--the even more bewildering change from an industrial to an information society, for example. It is fair to ask, for example, if we will be wise enough today to prevent area after area in our central cities from declining from prosperous business centers to rundown and depressed areas where jobs are disappearing at the same time when many people are in desperate need of work? We shall see, for today many of our cities are struggling with the same fundamental problems of providing basic water, sewer, fire and public safety services that small farm towns like Hoffman had to deal with in their day.

Today, some sociologists warn that the crowding of people together in cities has the potential of wearing away our individuality, and, indeed, many would agree that too many people today feel like very small spokes in huge wheels than they ever have before. Three or four generations ago when individual craftsmanship, small town merchandising, small farms, and small companies were the cornerstones of life, people enjoyed a greater feeling of independence than some do in modern societies. As the world is now, many areas of business enterprise are dominated by a relatively few large corporations, creating contexts where nobody feels indispensable and too many feel downright unnecessary.

It is sometimes jokingly said that if you really want to gauge your importance in the world, just stick your finger in a glass of water and then pull it out. What you see when you look in the glass will show how big a hole would be left behind if you were gone. If it is true that the feelings suggested by this saying have grown over the years since we left the small family farms of our fathers, then we are looking at one of the darker downsides of modern life in large cities today. The bigger the group, the less important any one person in that group can become to the whole. When we were a more dispersed and rural population, everybody felt more importance in his own place. Some of our former sense of time and place has been lost today, and more and more people seem to have problems dealing with reality. The root cause of their problem may be that they have more difficulty feeling the sense of belonging that people took for granted years ago in small farm towns like Hoffman.

Today, very few of us know (or even want to know) our neighbors like we used to. A family living just two houses away from any one of us might move out in the night and most of us would never even know they had left. In the smaller towns of Oklahoma's townsite days, that would not have happened. For better or worse, everybody knew everybody back then. Neighbors depended more on neighbors than they do today, and everybody meant something to someone. Living in a small town meant that people knew their neighbors, and neighbors knew that they would be missed if they left. This realization is neither maudlin nor provincial, and just thinking about what it suggests is enough to leave many of us with an uneasy awareness of how far away we are from having all the right answers for meeting the common emotional needs of people.

Recent public opinion polls indicate that two out of three Americans think the country is seriously off track in terms of moral, spiritual, and social order. The fraying of America's social fabric has become a major national concern, and studies have shown that as many as three out of four Americans agree with the assertion that "We are in moral and spiritual decline." According to Senator Daniel Patrick Moynihan some years back, we are currently caught up in a process of "defining deviancy down"--that is, of accepting as part of life (because we feel unable to do anything about it) the presence of beliefs, values, and lifestyles we once found to be against prevailing standards of decency, public order, and morality.

There are many who feel that we have lost our understanding of a proper balance between social rights and individual freedoms. We see today, for example, almost constant confrontations with almost everyone in authority: blacks against the white power structure, women against men and marriage, feminists against feminism, "gays" against "straight" society, children against parents, mothers against marriage, fathers against child support, citizens against the government, churchgoers against the church, students against universities, and so on an so on. Instead of sharing a culture of common good, it sometimes feels like we are caught up in a culture of constant complaint. From one perspective or another, almost everyone can claim to be a victim. Have-nots claim victimization at the hands of the successful, and crime is sometimes justified by the fact, real or imagined, that the criminal had an unhappy childhood. Sometimes it seems that the habits that we once most admired--habits such as thriftiness, industriousness, self-discipline, and personal commitment--seem to have all but disappeared.

The combined effects of these perceived societal problems, regardless of their root causes, has been to decrease our sense of optimism and to drain away our confidence in the future. And it is the young people of our society who have been the most vulnerable. Many of them are being deprived--like no previous generation--of the emotional comfort and moral nurturing that used to be provided by the traditional family. For many, instant gratification is the new order of the day, and unhealthy personal impulses are routinely stimulated by popular music and television, with other mass media not far behind. Television and music often seem to glorify everything that we used to find repulsive--violence, infidelity, drugs, drinking--and to dishonor everything we used to respect--religious conviction, marital commitment, respect for authority. No wonder people today often feel a need to look back to earlier days in search of a better way of life.

The disquieting sense of need some people feel today for higher public commitment to social and moral betterment is not a simple nostalgia for the greater simplicities of yesteryear. We know it is not possible to turn back the clock. But what many sense today is a profound and anxious desire to prevent further social decay. In our hearts we know that if the dysfunctional trends of recent years continue, the anxiety felt by many can turn into fear or even panic. And if fear ever comes to dominate social policy and our social behavior, reason and tolerance will be put at risk. Our society, in other words, could become like those we see today in the many troubled places of the world. This is the predicament we find ourselves in today, and it is one reason why many of us frequently feel a need to look back on the relatively quiet and simpler lives people lived in places like Hoffman Townsite.

PETITION FOR DISSOLUTION OF THE TOWN OF HOFFMAN

"Exhibit A"

TO THE BOARD OF TRUSTEES, TOWN OF HOFFMAN, OKMULGEE COUNTY,

STATE OF OKLAHOMA:

We, the undersigned citizens and legal voters of the State of
Oklahoma, County of Okmulgee, Town of Hoffman, respectfully request
the dissolution of the corporation of Hoffman for the following reasons:
We presently have an inadequate water system, inadequate maintenance
of streets, no fire protection, and lack of police power. Further,
we request that the question hereinafter stated be submitted to the
legal voters of the State of Oklahoma, County of Okmulgee, Town of
Hoffman, for their approval or rejection at a special town election,
to be held within thirty (30) days from the receipt of this petition,
and each for himself says: I have personally signed this petition; I
am a legal voter of the State of Oklahoma and of the County of Okmulgee,
Town of Hoffman; my residence and post office are clearly written after
my name. The time for filing this petition expires ninety (90) days
from March 11, 1966. The question we herewith submit to our fellow
voters is: "Shall the corporation of the Town of Hoffman be dissolved?"

W A R N I N G

"It is a felony for anyone to sign an initiative or referendum
petition with any name other than his own, or knowingly to sign his
name more than once for the measure, or to sign such petition when he
is not a legal voter."

*PETITION FOR THE DISSOLUTION OF THE TOWN OF
HOFFMAN – PAGE 1
APRIL 12, 1966*

NAME	ADDRESS
1. Lloyd Maxwell	Box 116
2. W. C. Stanton	Box 734
3. Jim Stanton	Box 724
4. Dorothy Stanton	Box 724
5. Mary Combs	P.O. Box 735
6. Pete Stanton	Box 726
7. Mrs. Joe Ritterhoff	Box 133 Hoffman, Okla.
8. Bea Stanton	Box 726 Hoffman Okla
9. Florence Stant	P.O. Box 734 Hoffman, Okla
10. J. D. Burney	Hoffman Okla
11. Violet Burney	Box 95 Hoffman, Okla
12. Joe L. Burney	Box 95 Hoffman, Okla
13. George M. ___	Hoffman Okla
14. Earnestine Myles (Mrs.)	P. O. Box 63 Hoffman Okla
15. Charlie Britt	P. O. Box 75 Hoffman Okla
16. Ishmael Britt	P O Box 75 Hoffman Okla
17. Edward Benedict	Box 61 Hoffman, Okla.
18. Willie Merril Benedict	Box 61 Hoffman, Okla
19. Johnnie Upshaw	Box 105 Hoffman Okla
20. Hope Smith	Hoffman Okla Box 96
21. Elza Daily	Hoffman Okla, Box 116
22. W. H. Daily	" "
23. Theodore Payne	P.O. Box 65 Hoffman
24. Lorene Payne	P. O. Box 65 Hoffman

PETITION FOR THE DISSOLUTION OF THE TOWN
OF HOFFMAN – PAGE 2
APRIL 12, 1966

25.	_[signature]_	hoffman 705
26.	_[signature]_	Hoffman Okla Box
27.	Don Ford	Hoffman Okla Box 733
28.	Rhoda Ford	Hoffman Okla Box 733
29.	_[signature]_	Hoffman Okla Box
30.	Von Kelly	Hoffman Okla Box 705
31.	Ruth _[illegible]_	Hoffman Okla Box 111
32.	Kenneth T. Cash	Box 717 Hoffman, Okla
33.	Juanita Cash	Box 717 Hoffman, Okla
34.	_[illegible] E. [illegible]_	Box 100 Hoffman, Okla
35.	Fred Brownfield	Box 692 Hoffman, Okla
36.	Inez Stanton	Box 734 Hoffman, Okla
37.	Shirley Combs	Gen Del Hoffman O
38.	Cecil Lewis	Hoffman Okla Box 8
39.	_[illegible] J. Million_	P.O. Box 126 Hoffman O
40.	_[illegible] Million_	P.O. Box 126 Hoffman O
41.	Nathaniel _[illegible]_	P.O. Box 84 Hoffman O
42.	Charline _[illegible]_	P.O. Box 84 Hoffman, Ok
43.		
44.		
45.		

"Exhibit A"

PETITION FOR THE DISSOLUTION OF THE TOWN
OF HOFFMAN – PAGE 3
APRIL 12, 1966

NOTICE

STATE OF OKLAHOMA)(
)(ss.
COUNTY OF OKMULGEE)(

TO THE LEGAL VOTERS RESIDING IN THE TOWN OF HOFFMAN, OKLAHOMA:

Notice is hereby given that pursuant to petition and application in due form signed by more than One-Third of the legal voters residing in the Town of Hoffman, Okmulgee County, Oklahoma, petitioning for an election to vote on the proposition of the dissolution of the Corporation of the Town of Hoffman, Oklahoma, and pursuant to Oklahoma Statutes, Title 11, Sections 982 and 976, a meeting of the legal voters of said town is hereby called for the 12 day of April, 1966, at 2:00 o'clock P. M. to be held in the auditorium of the Public School House at Hoffman, Oklahoma, and the business of such meeting shall be as aforesaid, to consider and vote at that time and place on the said following proposition, to-wit:

SHALL THE CORPORATION OF THE TOWN OF HOFFMAN BE DISSOLVED?

Virginia Owen
TOWN CLERK

Buster Ivary Tres
Glen England
Lonze Gresham

Trustees of the town of Hoffman, Oklahoma.

Subscribed and sworn to before me this 1st day of April, 1966.

Lillian Davis
Lillian Davis, Notary Public

My commission expires 11-2-69.

*PETITION FOR THE DISSOLUTION OF THE TOWN
OF HOFFMAN – PAGE 4
APRIL 12, 1966*

PROPOSITION

SHALL THE CORPORATION OF THE TOWN
OF HOFFMAN, IN OKMULGEE COUNTY,
STATE OF OKLAHOMA, BE DISSOLVED?

"YES"- "NO"

INSTRUCTIONS: Write in the square the word
"yes" if you favor dissolution. Write in
the square the word "no" if you oppose
dissolution.

PETITION FOR THE DISSOLUTION OF THE TOWN
OF HOFFMAN – PAGE 5
APRIL 12, 1966

AFFIDAVIT OF TOWN ELECTION
DISSOLVING CORPORATION

2097

STATE OF OKLAHOMA)(
)(ss.
COUNTY OF OKMULGEE)(

This is to certify that pursuant to a petition presented to
the Town Clerk and Trustees of the Town of Hoffman, Okmulgee
County, Oklahoma, bearing the signatures of more than one-
third of the legal voters of said town (Exhibit A), and pursuant to Notices duly published and posted according to law
(Exhibits B and C), a meeting of the voters of the Town of
Hoffman, Oklahoma, was called to order at 2:00 P.M. o'clock
on the 12th. day of April, 1966, in the auditorium of the
Public School at Hoffman and the proposition as follows was
voted on in accordance with said notices: "Shall the Corporation of the Town of Hoffman be Dissolved."

This is to further certify that the proposition carried on a
vote of "yes" or "no" by a vote as follows:

"Yes"--Forty-three (43) votes
"No"---Nineteen (19) votes

the same being more than two-fifths (2/5) of the registered
voters of said town. (Exhibit 1-A)

THEREFORE, pursuant to Oklahoma Statutes, Title 11, Section
982 this is to finally certify that on the 12th. day of October,
1966, same being a date six months from the date hereof, said
Corporation of the Town of Hoffman, Okmulgee County, Oklahoma,
shall be dissolved and shall cease to exist.

Buster Ivory Tree

Virginia Queen
_____
Town Clerk

Glen Poland

Lonza Gresham
_____
Trustees

Subscribed and sworn to before me this ___12th___ day of
___April___, 1966.

Lillian Davis
_____
Lillian Davis, Notary Public

My commission expires 11-2-69.

*PETITION FOR THE DISSOLUTION OF THE TOWN
OF HOFFMAN – PAGE 6
APRIL 12, 1966*

1975 photograph of the delipidated remains of the C. E. Lackey store constructed in 1934. Years later, the building burned to the ground. After that, a community center was built on the slab of the old store. The center is still in operation today.

1975 photograph of the east side of the Main Street of Hoffman

*Remains of the W. A. Anthony's Store,
which once housed the Hoffman Post Office*

*1970's photograph of the delipidated remains
of Hoffman's WPA High School and Gymnasium*

An abandoned home in Hoffman

Former home of C. R. Martin at Hoffman,
abandoned for years, then demolished

CHAPTER VIII

THE
FUTURE OF HOFFMAN

For several years following the vote in 1966 to dissolve the Corporation of the Town of Hoffman, citizens of Hoffman relied on the County of Okmulgee and the State of Oklahoma to provide street and road maintenance, police and fire protection, and other essential services. Before long, however, dissatisfaction arose over the quality and quantity of support that was being delivered. To more effectively cope with the necessity of providing basic public services, the few hundred remaining residents of Hoffman voted in 1968 to reincorporate their town.

It took until 1973, however, before any substantial progress was made in terms of improving local public services. In that year, Hoffman received the first of a series of community redevelopment grants offered by the federal government through programs of the Department of Housing and Urban Development. By means of various grant applications over the next few years, a new gas system, water system, some housing rehabilitation, storm and flood control systems, and new streets and bar ditches were made possible. Additional applications may lead to more funding for the rehabilitation of decaying homes and for the replacement of aging septic tank systems, both of which are critical needs.

THE GENTLE GIANT,
LAKE EUFAULA

Any substantial future growth that may take place in the town of Hoffman or in its general proximity is likely to be in some way related to the existence of Oklahoma's "Gentle Giant," Lake Eufaula, which is a major draw to the surrounding area. Parts of the lake extend to just a few miles from the edge of Hoffman Townsite. This large and beautiful man-made body of water draws in many visitors and, more significantly for Hoffman and other towns in its vicinity, an annually increasing number of vacation-home owners and retirees. In the promotional material that was designed to promote the development, follows, the overall project as well as the lake per se were described as follows:

Authorized by the federal River and Harbor Act of 1946, Eufaula was started in December of 1956 and completed eight years later. The project was finished in February and dedicated by President Lyndon B. Johnson on September 25 of 1964. Designed by and built under the supervision of the Army Corps of Engineers at a cost of $121 million, Lake Eufaula is a key unit in the project for comprehensive development of the Arkansas River and its tributaries. The drainage area above the dam encompasses about 48,000 square miles and the surface area of the lake at the top of the area flood control pool is 143,700 acres.

The Eufaula dam is located on the Canadian River about 27 miles upstream from its confluence with the Arkansas River. It is located about 28 miles northwest of Hoffman and about 12 miles east of the town of Eufaula. It is a rolled earthfill embankment dam with a total length of 3,200 feet including the powerhouse intake and concrete gate spillway. The normal power pool contains 2,330,000 acre-feet for powerhead and water supply storage with a surface area of 102,200 acres.

Of the hundreds of such lakes in the United States, Eufaula is the 15th largest. In its region, it is second in size only to Lake Texhoma on the Oklahoma-Texas border. Located in the center of eastern Oklahoma, most of the 600-mile shoreline of this huge body of water lies in McIntosh County, within the boundaries of the old Creek Indian Nation. Other parts of the lake are in Haskell, Pittsburg, Okmulgee, Muskogee and Latimer Counties.

Eufaula is a multi-purpose lake designed to provide flood control, hydroelectric power, water supplies and recreational benefits to a wide area. In addition, it also aids the McClellan-Kerr Navigation System of the region by assisting and maintaining regulated flows downstream to the Arkansas river. As a flood control system, it was estimated that by as early as 1986 the lake had prevented as much as $46 million in damage by storing flood waters in its nearly 48,000 square mile drainage area. In addition, its powerplant had supplied over 3.1 billion kilowatt hours of electrical energy to the Southwestern Power Administration for distribution and over $16.3 million in revenue had been returned to the U. S. Treasury from the sale of this power.

Twenty-one park areas have been developed by the Army Corps of Engineers around the lake. Improved access roads lead into the park areas, all of which have boat launching ramps. In addition, the State of Oklahoma developed two beautiful lodges--Arrowhead and Fountainhead—to make guestrooms, deluxe cottages and convention facilities, as well as fishing docks, service docks, golf courses, picnic areas, campgrounds and airparks available to visitors.

The major camping sites and picnic areas around the lake are furnished with restrooms, parking areas, picnic shelters, drinking water, charcoal grills, and trash containers. During the summer season, on weekends, various interpretive programs are made available at selected camping areas. The subject matter includes wildlife, recreation, resource management, and other topics of interest to outdoorsmen. Some of the numerous concessions around the lake include fishing docks which are heated in the winter and air-conditioned in the summer. In 1979, for example, a year in which patronage studies were conducted, 6.4 million persons visited Corps facilities alone.

Fishing makes up a large portion of the recreational activities on Lake Eufaula. Year-round fishing is very good. Striped bass, largemouth bass, white bass, crappie, catfish, walleye and numerous sunfish provide most of the sport fishing. To enhance the success of fish and wildlife, the Oklahoma Department of Wildlife Conservation and Corps of Engineers work cooperatively to improve fish habitat by construction and location of brush shelters and controlling sources of pollution entering the lake.

Project lands are open for public hunting, except for the developed park areas and the lands in the vicinity of the dam and other project structures. The principle game species include bobwhite quail, deer, cottontail rabbit, squirrel, duck, geese and mourning dove. Hunting licenses and fishing are regulated by State and Federal laws, and the same licenses are required as in other parts of Oklahoma. Public hunting maps showing both Corps and State areas open for hunting are available from the Eufaula Project Office at the dam or the Tulsa District Office.

By land or water, natural beauty abounds in every nook and cranny of the lake area. Boaters on Lake Eufaula are continually awed by the change in shoreline scenery, especially its meandering chains of bays and channels set in rolling prairie backed by many lofty hills.

Four-lane highway access is excellent in the area. Interstate 40 is open east and west and both the Indian Nation and Muskogee Turnpikes serve areas to the north and south. State Highway 9 and black top or gravel roads offer many scenic views of the lake. Driving down U. S. Highway 69 from Checotah to McAlester, the waters of the lake can be seen for miles on both sides of the highway and, even then, only a small portion of this gigantic lake is visible. Scenic drives around the lake are especially beautiful in the early spring, and in the fall the beautiful landscape of color is fantastic. Impressive views of the lake at almost every curve of the road makes a tour around the lake a memorable trip in any season.

Visitors with knowledge of the area know that most of the 600-mile shoreline of Lake Eufaula lies within the boundaries of the old Creek Indian Nation and that part of the southern portion lies in the old Choctaw Indian Nation. Many of the reminders of the colorful history of this area--including Indian life, outlaw gangs, and Civil War battles--remain for visitors to see.

The Battle of Honey Springs, the largest and most important of the battles fought during the Civil War in Oklahoma, took place on July 17, 1863, on a site about 20 miles east of Hoffman. Honey Springs Depot was a supply station for the Confederate forces. Supplies were brought in from Fort Smith, Arkansas, and from Fort Washita, Fort Cobb, Fort Arbuckle, and Boggy Depot. Gunpowder was sent there from Mexico. It was at Elk Creek in this location that a Union force of 3,000 men commanded by General J. G. Blunt attacked a Confederate force commanded by General D. H. Cooper. The superior arms and equipment of the Union troops forced the Confederates to withdraw after suffering heavy losses. The battleground site is presently owned by the Oklahoma Historical Society.

The waters Lake Eufaula also cross the old Texas Road, over which in the 1830s more than a thousand covered wagons rolled each week as settlers moved from the east into Texas. The much-used trail was the forerunner of the present-day U.S. Highway 69. When the Missouri, Kansas & Texas Railroad--the "Katy"-- built the first rail lines southward across Indian Territory in 1872, it also followed the route of the Texas Road.

Eufaula, the county seat of McIntosh County and former Record Town for Recording District Number 12 of Indian Territory, was named after one of the historic Creek Indian villages in the Creeks' old homeland in Alabama. Just a half mile east of Eufaula was the site of North Fork Town, settled by the Creeks shortly after their arrival in this area in 1836. The Texas Road and a branch of the California Road crossed at North Fork Town, making it a center of traffic. This important tribal community was the scene of the treaty-making between the Confederates and the Creeks, Choctaws, and Chickasaws in 1861. It is now inundated by the waters of Lake Eufaula.

Those who visit the area can treat themselves to a historical feast if they visit the Creek Indian Council House and Museum which stands in the middle of the square in downtown Okmulgee. Exhibits include Indian murals and paintings, pioneer history and archeology.

Near the north end of Eufaula Dam was the home of Belle Starr, the fabled woman outlaw of early Indian territorial days. Here was the hideout of her gang, and at times of other outlaws such the Youngers and Jessie and Frank James. Northeast of Eufaula is the site of the Asbury Mission, a boarding school established by the Methodist Episcopal Church in 1849 in cooperation with the Creek Indian Tribal Council. The original buildings burned in 1889 and were rebuilt by the Creeks in 1892. The Indian Journal, located at Eufaula, is the oldest surviving newspaper in Oklahoma. It was founded in Muskogee in 1876 as a Creek tribal organ. It was once edited by Alexander Posey, a famous Creek poet and statesman.

One of the most famous landmarks of the area has vanished beneath the waters of Lake Eufaula. Standing Rock, which stood 63 feet above the waters of the Canadian River five miles east of Eufaula, was noted as a fishing spot by early-day settlers. Standing Rock was first recorded by early day Spanish explorers. Spanish symbols carved on the rock were believed by some to have pointed to the location of buried treasure. The rock also was mentioned in notes of Captain Bonneville, who led an expedition there from Fort Gibson, Oklahoma, in 1830.

The City of Checotah is located at the northern end of Lake Eufaula situated on the intersections of Interstate 40 and U. S. Highway 69. Teeming with history, the town was named after Samuel Checote, a full-blood Creek Indian who was born near Fort Mitchell, Alabama, in 1819. He came to Indian Territory with his parents in 1829. Under the influence of the great missionary, John Harrell, he attended missionary schools and in 1852 was licensed to preach by the Methodist Church. He continued to preach for the rest of his life.

Checotah was first established between 1870-1872. It was first a small telegraph office, but not long thereafter the M.K.&T. Railroad arrived in the area. By 1883, there were a few businesses at the location, including the General Motel and the Subscription School, along with some residential shacks. Its First Baptist Church was started with five members in 1898. The Checotah Enquirer newspaper was established in 1902. On November 16, 1907, the old Checotah, Creek Nation, Indian Territory, became the new Checotah, McIntosh County, Oklahoma, and by 1919 Checotah had three banks and a population of 4,000.

The town of McAlester is located on the southern banks of Lake Eufaula. It began in 1870 as a tent store at the crossroads of two well-traveled Indian Territory roads, the California Trail and the Texas Road. The owner of the tent store was James J. McAlester, after whom the town was named. Today it is a city with a population of well over 20,000. Former Oklahoma Governor George Nigh and ex-Speaker of the House Carl Albert have been residents of the McAlester.

Sadly, the two lodges did not draw in enough guests to be financially successful. Fountainhead, as comfortable and attractive as it once was, eventually had to be demolished. Arrowhead was taken over by the State of Oklahoma and turned into a special purpose rehabilitation facility. The remainder of the facilities developed at Lake Eufaula, however, continue to function as intended.

PROSPECTS FOR HOFFMAN

Today, the spot on the map of Okmulgee County in the State of Oklahoma called Hoffman is a small community consisting of a handful of residences, a city hall and rural fire department, and a few churches pastored by part-time preachers from out-of-town. It is a tiny dot on maps of the area, and those who look at it might be tempted to believe that it has been long forgotten. That is not the case, however; memories of what Hoffman once was and what it represented live on in the hearts and minds of former residents, their descendants and students of the area, even though they live may far away in other towns and states.

Finding the wherewithal to maintain essential public services in Hoffman will remain an uphill economic struggle, just as it was in the early days of the townsite. Given enough time, however, and more new arrivals interested in living around beautiful Lake Eufaula, Hoffman may once again, like the Phoenix from the ashes, rise to become a thriving country town. There are those who would love to see the day!

For the time being, however, Hoffman is likely to remain the small dot that it is on maps of the mostly rural landscape of Okmulgee County. In its location about eight miles from the town of Henryetta (which is itself located about 70 miles south of Tulsa near the intersection of the Indian Nation Turnpike and Interstate Highway 40), only those who really want to see the place have a reason to go there today. Originally incorporated in McIntosh County in a portion of what once was known as the Indian Territory, the town is not visible from any heavily traveled road and the average person would certainly have to be looking for it to find it. And, once found, it would be clear in a minute that there is not much left of it to be seen.

Nevertheless, what does remain of old Hoffman is more than enough to evoke some powerful images among those who have studied events that took place there in years past. Many lives were touched by the little town, and micro versions of many of the episodes of human activity that make up the history of the State of Oklahoma, and, indeed, the very history of our country, were lived out in this small place. The story of its struggles makes us think of common roots and basic values and serves as a reminder of the fact that the things we have in common are far more important and meaningful than any of our differences. Knowing that many of those who came before us lived through experiences like those that played out at Hoffman is what makes the story of places like it so fascinating!

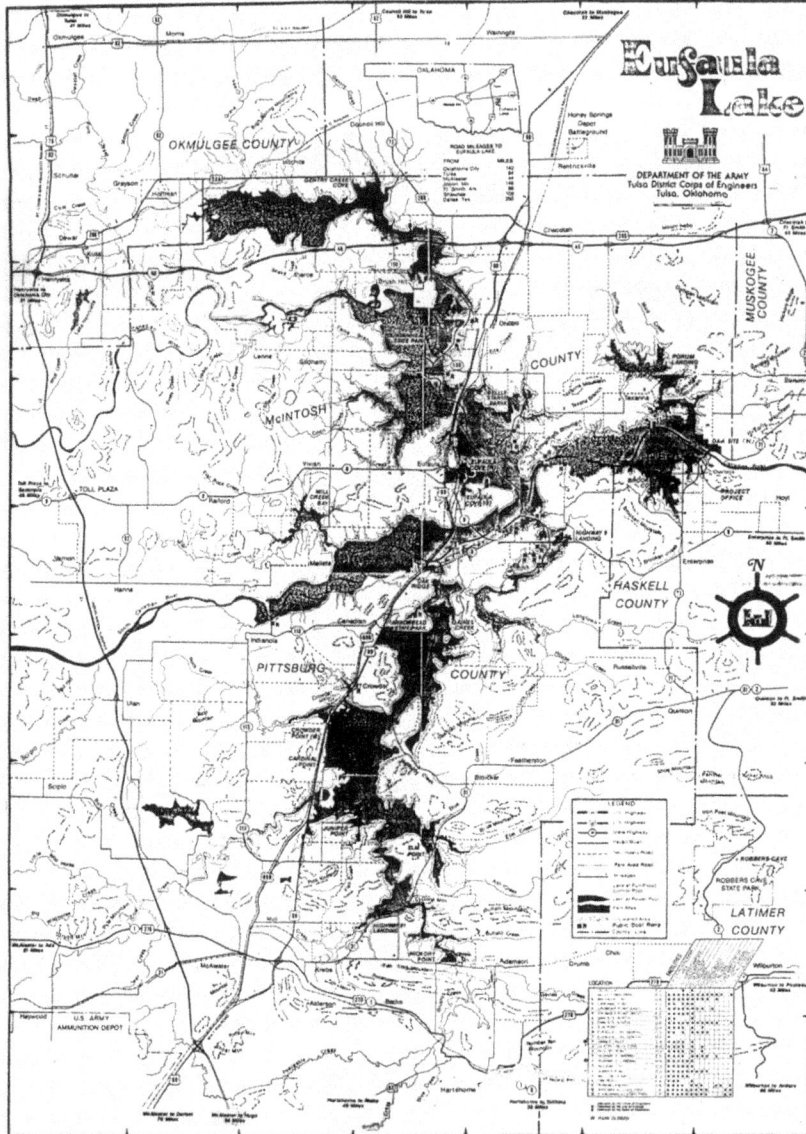

*SHORELINE MAP OF
"THE GENTLE GIANT," LAKE EUFAULA*

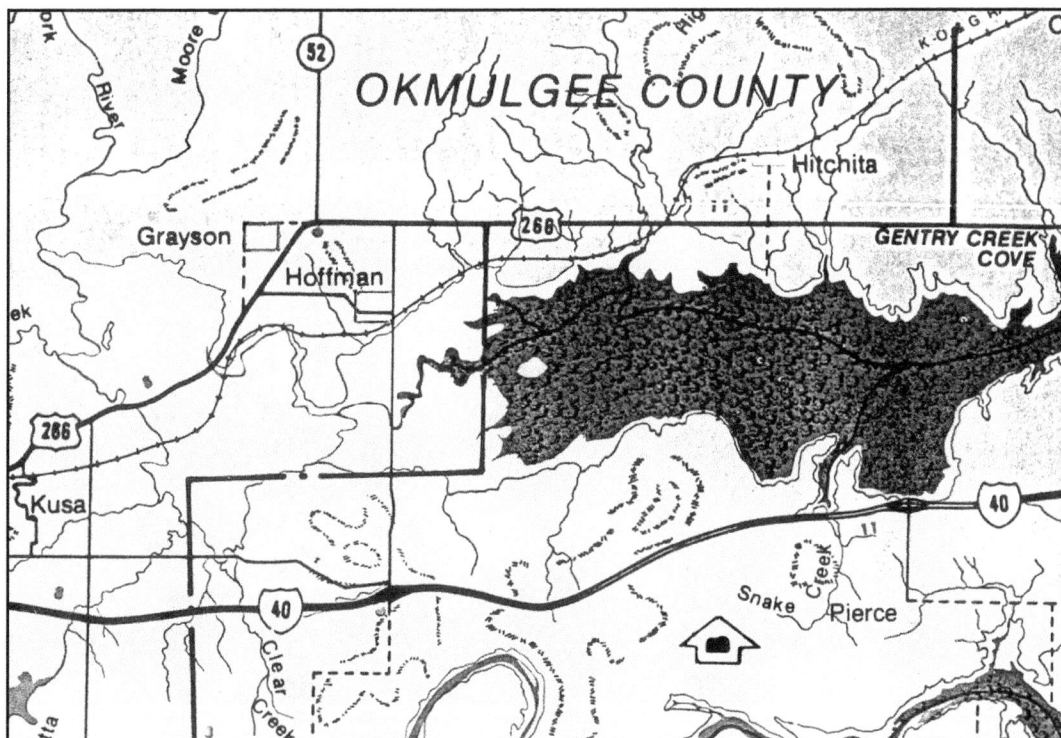

Map showing the proximity of Lake Eufaula to Hoffman

The dam at Lake Eufaula

*Allen Bridgewater, Mike Martin, Don Harriman, and Paul Hutchison
at the 1993 Hoffman School and Town Reunion*

*Arley Anthony, Mike Martin and Chuff Nicholson
at the 1994 Hoffman School and Town Reunion*

1994 HOFFMAN REUNION GROUP

FRONT ROW: Mary (Edwards) Martin, Blanche (Hutchison) (Didlake) Lambert, Fern (Howk) Rhodes, Charles Lackey, Jr., June Lackey, Gladys (Moffett) Rawlings, Sybil Geasland, and Mike Martin.

MIDDLE ROW: Judith (Lackey) Southerland, Grace (Porter) Moore, Lois (Porter) Hood, Inez (Lackey) Mathis, Brunell (Lackey) Moore, Billye (Peters) Clark, Emma Lou (Parker) Quinton, Marie (Brown) Hutchison, Joyce (Bowden) Scroggins, Garnie (Jefferson) Ritter, Dorothy (Porter) (Edwards) Tuley, Bonnie (Sessions) Tennant, and Allene (Geasland) Eckfeldt.

BACK ROW: Robert Martin, Don Harriman, Rex Burney, Arley Anthony, Tom Barron, H. Lee "Buck" Peaden, Paul Hutchison, Jack Collins, Goldia (Porter) Collins, Wilma (Lippard) Rawlings, Kenneth Sessions, Darlene Sessions, and Jack Scroggins.

REFERENCES

BOOKS

Baird, W. David (Editor). _A Creek Warrior for the Confederacy: The Autobiography of Chief G. W. Grayson._
    (Norman: The University of Oklahoma Press, 1988)

Beaver, R. Pierce. _Church, State, and the American Indians._
    (St. Louis: Concordia Publishing House, 1966)

Berkhofer, Robert F. _Salvation and the Savage: An Analysis of Protestant Missions and American Indian Responses._
    (Lexington: University of Kentucky Press, 1965)

Berkin, Carol and Wood, Leonard. _Land of Promise: A History of the United States From 1865._
    (Glenview, Illinois: Scott, Foresman and Company, 1986)

Boren, Lyle H. _Who Is Who In Oklahoma._
    (Guthrie: Co-operative Publishing Company, 1935)

Debo, Angie. _A History of the Indians of the United States._
    (Norman: University of Oklahoma Press, 1970)

Debo, Angie. _The Road to Disappearance._
    (Norman: University of Oklahoma Press, 1941)

Eichholz, Alice (Editor). _Ancestry's Redbook: American State, County and Town Sources._
    (Salt Lake City: Ancestry Publishing, 1989)

Foreman, Carolyn Thomas. _Oklahoma Imprints: A History of Printing in Oklahoma Before Statehood, 1835-1907._
    (Norman: University of Oklahoma Press, 1936)

Foreman, Grant. _The Five Civilized Tribes._
    (Norman: University of Oklahoma Press, 1934)
Green, Michael D. _The Politics of Indian Removal._

(Lincoln: University of Nebraska Press, 1982)

Hastain, E. *Hastain's Township Plats of the Creek Nation*.
(Muskogee: Bureau of Indian Affairs)

Martin, Mickey J. *My Indian Territory School*.
(The Fowble Press)

Martin, Mickey J. *A Photographic History of Hoffman School in Okmulgee County, Oklahoma*. (The Fowble Press)

Miller, Francis Trevelyan. *The Photographic History of the Civil War*.
(New York: The Blue and Gray Press, 1911)

Nelson, Albert M. (Editor) *Who's Who in America*.
(Chicago: A. N. Marquis Company, 1938-39 Edition)

Okmulgee Genealogical Society. *Okmulgee County, Oklahoma, Cemetery Records*.
(Okmulgee: Okmulgee Genealogical Society, 1974)

Shirk, George H. *Oklahoma Place Names*.
(Norman: University of Oklahoma Press, 1974)

Sifakis, Stewart. *Who Was Who In the Civil War*.
(New York: Facts on File Inc., 1988)

Theoburn, Joseph B. *A Standard History of Oklahoma*.
(New York, Chicago: American Historical Society, 1916)

Waldman, Carl. *Atlas of the North American Indian*.
(New York, Oxford: Facts on file Public, 1985)

Wright, J. Leitch, Jr. *Creeks and Seminoles: The Destruction and Regeneration of the Muscogulge People*.
(Lincoln: University of Nebraska Press, 1987)

ARTICLES

_____. "The Crazy Snake Uprising of 1909; A Red, Black or White Affair?" *Arizona and the West*. Vol. 20, No. 4, Winter, 1978, p. 2

_____. "From Sod House to Brigadier General." *Harlow's Weekly*. AP 2, H28, V14, No.9, September 5, 1917, p. 11.

_____. "Selection of U. S. Senators."
Sturm's. V4, No.1, p. 16.

NEWSPAPERS

Guy, Steven B. "Tales of Hoffman." The Morris News. November 1, 1990, p. 10.

Hood, Helena. "California Crazy." The Hoffman School Herald. November 25, 135, p. 1.

Hood, Helena. "Gymnasium Project." The Hoffman School Herald. November 25, 1935, p. 1.

Johnston, Kelly. "Federal Funds Helping Small Community." South County Super Circulation Edition, The Henryetta Daily Free-Lance. Wednesday, July 12, 1978, p. 1.

O'Bleness, O. E. "Hoffman." The Hoffman Herald. Vol. I, April 5, 1906, p. 3.

Tharp, Bill. "Hoffman Tornado Victims Express Gratitude to American Red Cross." Henryetta Daily Free-Lance. February 26, 1961, p. 1.

Zellner, Wanda Bowden. "Glory Days of Hoffman Recalled by Graduate." Okmulgee Daily Times. Mainstream Edition, August 7, 1991, p. 6.

_____ "Pioneer Rodeo Showman Born, Resides In City." Okmulgee Daily Times. Mainstream Edition, April 17, 1991, p. 6.

GOVERNMENT PUBLICATIONS

"Documents on the Emigration of the Indians," SD 512, 23d Congress, 1st Session, Serials 245, 246.

"Hoffman School Nomination Form, National Registry of Historic Places, National Park Service, United States Department of the Interior," Oklahoma State Historical Society

"Historical Records Survey, Works Progress Administration," A List of the Records of the State of Oklahoma. Oklahoma City: Historical Records Survey, 1938.

"Railroads of Oklahoma," Survey Division, Department of Highways, State of Oklahoma, January 1, 1970.

"Enrollment Cards of the Five Civilized Tribes, 1898-1914," Records of the Bureau of Indian Affairs, Record Group 75.

INDEX

ALSO BY
MICKEY J. "MIKE" MARTIN

BRYANT: A CREEK INDIAN NATION TOWNSITE
ISBN 9780963827944 (Hardback)
ISBN 9781478198956 (Paperback)
LCCN 2012942764

MY INDIAN TERRITORY SCHOOL
ISBN 9780963827968 (Hardback)
ISBN 9781470131098 (Paperback)
LCCN 2012932399

MOCK'S BAD STOMP
ISBN 9780963827975 (Hardback)
ISBN 9780963827982 (Paperback)
ISBN 9780963827999 (EPUB)
LCCN 2021909316

THE LADY LUCK: STORY OF THE USS LST-864
ISBN 978-0-9638279-5-2 (Hardback)
LCCN 2003095571

$$\Omega$$